D0777549

WILL TRAVEL FOR VEGAN FOOD

"Part Cheryl Strayed, part Elizabeth Gilbert, Kristin is able to beautifully blend travel, adventure, and good plant-based food into an epic and interesting tale."
— Paul Jarvis, bestselling author of *Everything I Know*

"Take the road trip of a lifetime with Kristin's brilliant tome on her journey across America in search of great vegan food. Join her in the passenger seat as she not only eats the best food of her life, but also faces unexpected twists and turns, falls in love, embarks on thrilling adventures, and discovers who she really is and what she wants her life to be. *Will Travel for Vegan Food* is heartwarming, laugh-out-loud funny, and full of suspense—and will inspire each reader to follow their heart and create the life of their dreams. Whether you're a die-hard foodie, an armchair traveler, or someone who just enjoys a good story, you'll love Kristin's debut novel. I can't wait for more."
— Colleen Holland, Co-Founder of *VegNews Magazine*

"*Will Travel For Vegan Food* is a candid and adventurous journey of a woman finding the courage to break free from what she fears most—a life of mediocrity. Her entrepreneurial endeavor is inspiring and shows us that life is a journey, and so is finding and living your passion and compassion."
— Jenny Brown, Co-Founder & Executive Director of Woodstock Farm Sanctuary, and author of *The Lucky Ones*

"Kristin's journey is not only one of inspiration but also of pure joy! Travel is one of the most enriching experiences in life, and travel while searching for incredible vegan food is my absolute fave! Kudos to Kristin for embarking on this adventure and sharing it with all of us!"
— Carolyn Scott-Hamilton, founder of *The Healthy Voyager*

"[Kristin's memoir] was one of those adventures that shaped a life in such a way that only those who have followed a quest such as this can reflect with deep sighs, wide smiles, and flashbacks of the senses as we take each step into her next restaurant or bite from the next great dish. It left me wanting and waiting to meet, eat, and laugh with the next joyful character Kristin encountered. This book is real, passionate, and shows that we all should take our adventurous natures and push them forward to achieve the quests of our passions! This book is the millennial version of *Eat Pray Love!*"
—Danny Boome, host of *Good Food America*,
Recipe Rehab, & Rescue Chef

"An adventurous, nomadic journey of exploring vegan cuisine, following your dreams, moving outside your comfort zone, trusting yourself, trusting the universe, and most of all, learning that there is nothing more important than self-love. Entertaining, educational, and inspiring."
—Grace Van Berkum, R.H.N., Vegan, Plant-Powered Nutritionist

"Quit your job, buy a used van, and spend 18 months driving around the country in search of vegan food? If you've ever felt the itch to drop everything and... well... live, then Kristin's story will remind you of why. Travel, food, love, and the life lessons disguised as "what was I thinking?" missteps, *Will Travel for Vegan Food* will leave you itching to finally make your own crazy adventure happen."
—Matt Frazier, author of *No Meat Athlete*

KRISTIN M. LAJEUNESSE

WILL TRAVEL FOR VEGAN FOOD

Kristin Lajeunesse is founder of and blogger for the award-winning website Will Travel for Vegan Food. In September 2011, the New York native began traveling throughout the US in an effort to eat at and write about every single all-vegan establishment she can find. Eighteen of those early consecutive travel months were spent living out of a renovated sports van affectionately named Gerty. Almost immediately after beginning her journey, Kristin discovered a deep passion for nomadic and unconventional living, and has since chosen to maintain a mobile lifestyle, indefinitely. As of July 2014, Kristin met her goal of visiting and eating in each of the 50 states. A self-employed business and lifestyle strategist, Kristin now works with small business owners and entrepreneurs looking to turn their passions into profitable careers. Kristin is also a founding member of the Vegan Weddings HQ website and the Unabridged Addiction podcast. She has a Master of Arts in Integrated Marketing Communication from Emerson College. Follow her travels and business adventures on wtfveganfood.com and kristinlajeunesse.com.

WILL TRAVEL
FOR vegan FOOD

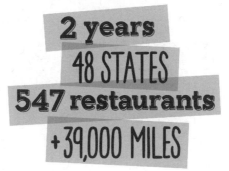

2 years
48 STATES
547 restaurants
+39,000 MILES

A Young Woman's Solo Van-Dwelling Mission
to Break Free, Find Food & Make Love

KRISTIN M. LAJEUNESSE

Vegan Publishers | Danvers, Massachusetts

*Some names have been changed in this book
to protect the privacy of the individuals involved.*

Will Travel for Vegan Food:
A Young Woman's Solo Van-Dwelling Mission to Break
Free, Find Food, & Make Love

Published by:
Vegan Publishers, Danvers, MA
www.veganpublishers.com

Cover and book design: Jacki Graziano

Printed in the United States of America on
100% recycled paper

ISBN 978-1-940184-10-4

For Christopher Zahka

———————

For my parents, Jan and Dave,
and for my brother, Josh

AUTHOR'S NOTE

THE FACTS Each chapter of this book is based on my personal recollection of the journey in addition to notes I kept in a journal, previously written blog posts on wtfveganfood.com, email exchanges, text messages, Facebook messages, and thousands of photos that chronicled the time, placement, and memories of specific locations, events, and conversations. Further, I consulted with a number of the people mentioned in the book.

THE FOOD Unless explicitly noted, all food and meals mentioned in the book are, to my knowledge, completely vegan (i.e., free of all meats, dairy, eggs, and honey). At times when the traditional use of a word is used—for example, "chicken" or "cheese"—it is a vegan version of the food item, unless otherwise stated. Please note that this is neither a cookbook nor a travel guide. However, more details on the food and restaurants from the journey, including countless photos, can be found on wtfveganfood.com and on the following social networks under the username "wtfveganfood": Instagram, Facebook, YouTube, and Twitter.

THE STORIES Most of the names and descriptions of people included in this book are real. I chose to change a few names and details in order to protect the identities of some. One of the biggest challenges writing this book was having to leave out many great stories, beautiful people, and amazing places. Some aspects of the journey were omitted if they did not have a significant impact on the narrative as it unfolded in this book. I met hundreds of incredible people who gifted me with immeasurable experiences; it was impossible to include every single one. I am incredibly grateful to each of you who helped me through this. You know who you are. Please know that your kindness and support did not go unnoticed.

CONTENTS

part one

CHAPTER 1

ALL FOR SOMETHING

"I'm sorry, but there are aspects of your personality that make me not want to be intimate with you," Nate said, lying on his right side, back toward me and breath just inches from the tote bags that lined the inside wall of the van. They held things like books we couldn't part with, random gadgets and their chords, some clothing, and other miscellaneous items we probably didn't need to have with us inside living quarters the size of a small walk-in closet.

It was October 27th and it was the day before my 29th birthday. It was an exceptionally cold night to be sleeping in a vehicle parked on a residential side street in Allston, Massachusetts— next to someone I'd met only three months earlier.

We had just finished our nightly ritual of 'closing up the van' by drawing together a set of blackout curtains that hung snugly from a piece of taut wire, the two drapes pieced together by vertically adhesed strips of Velcro. That set of curtains separated the driver and passenger seats from the back of the van where, two months earlier, Nate had pulled out both rows of bucket seats and, with the help of my dad, built in the platform bed, extra battery storage, and a secret safety lockbox. Nate had also hand cut and glued Velcro onto blackout curtains that lined all the windows in the back of the van. We opened them during the day while driving, closed them if we left the van for more than a few hours, and used them to insulate our incognito shelter at night.

Nate lay motionless beside me, our bodies buried beneath separate sleeping bags, topped with layers of shared blankets. I, in a ski hat and gloves, felt paralyzed and angry. I felt afraid and in love. I remained on my back staring up into the darkness, hyperaware of Nate's deep silence. It seemed hard to breathe. The air was still and I was lost for words. My heart and throat felt pinched, like they were being squeezed by giant tongs. I pictured Neo reaching into my chest and magically releasing the pressure, like that time he removed a bullet from Trinity's heart.

Earlier that day, we celebrated the placement of our first "Will Travel for Vegan Food was here" window decal at Veggie Galaxy in Boston. Nate and I had both been living in Boston before the trip began, and the restaurant was newly open— about two months—so it seemed a fitting starting point for what would lead to hundreds of placed decals across the country.

I was over the moon that a restaurant had agreed to place one of the decals on their street-facing picture window. Nate snapped a photo of me standing bundled up outside the restaurant, hands pressed karate chopping-style against the glass, on either side of the decal, showcasing it with a Vanna White flair.

It was Nate's idea to order a box of these three by four-inch, brown-with-white-lettering static cling decals. I agreed it was a terrific way to leave a little something behind at each of our stops.

I watched my breath escape above me once more before turning onto my left side. The chilly air swooped beneath the blankets as I moved, and I felt Nate's body inch farther away.

Now back-to-back, with an agonizing two-inch gap between us, I closed my eyes tightly, releasing a few silent tears. I tucked my freezing nose into the sleeping bag, pressed my cheek deeper into the pillow, and tortured myself to sleep by reminiscing about the Mach 20 courtship and its equally speedy decline that had brought us here.

It would be another three months before I'd have the courage to tell Nate that I think it'd be best if I continued on without him.

It was almost exactly one year earlier that it all seemed so impossible—scammy even. But I took the words that sat there in front of me on the computer screen as a directive, taunting me with their profound intangibility.

I spent months devouring blog post after book, absorbing unbelievable stories about people who make a living off of digital businesses they created via single websites, learning about people who were traveling all over the world, stopping to work wherever they pleased, whenever they wanted, so long as they had an internet connection. Could it be true? Is it *really* doable, or just a means to sell me something?

I closed the browser window for artofnonconformity.com, set the computer to sleep mode, and pushed into the desk with both hands, rolling the cushy chair backwards. I collected my purse from under the desk and let my coworker Katie know that I was headed out for my lunch break.

While walking to the elevator, I glanced down into my bag to see the orange book cover of Tim Ferriss' *The 4-Hour Workweek* sitting unassumingly inside. I couldn't wait to continue reading about the "new rich." I had already finished reading *Crush It!* by Gary Vaynerchuk and was feeling more inspired than ever to start my own business. But what? I was lost on ideas, though

I couldn't stop thinking about traveling indefinitely, working from the road, and living with fewer possessions.

My parents have so many things. A house FULL of things. Things they don't use—my things, their things, my brother's things. My grandparents collected lots of things too. From my earliest memory, I recall their tiny house in Troy, New York, overflowing with hidden treasures, newspapers from decades passed, dolls, toys, and trinkets from my mom's childhood. I understand the reasons for collecting things, and the sentimental value in keeping that stuff around. But I was also having trouble with the idea of purchasing a home that I would start filling with *my* things.

Tim's and Gary's books are what led me to the likes of Chris Guillebeau, Corbett Barr, Adam Baker, Pat Flynn, and Marie Forleo, among others. I'd come home from my nine-to-five job, work a few hours for my part-time job, and then spend the rest of the night and early mornings reading about full-time nomads, van-dwellers, lifestyle designers, entrepreneurs, and game changers. The wheels started turning, and I found myself feverishly scribbling notes and daydreaming about becoming a real business owner, a real entrepreneur. A female entrepreneur! It sounded fancy—luxurious, even.

It wasn't just the idea of designing my life around what I most loved, or even working for myself. What really pulled me in was how different my current life path was to the one I now felt deeply drawn to.

What I told myself about growing up included going to college, then to graduate school, landing a stable job, buying a home, and starting a family, all while spending the rest of my life paying off student loans and mortgage debt. Once I'd reached the 'stable job' part of equation, including having racked up well over $60,000 in student loans from grad school, I was definitely not feeling the homeowner or family-starter end of things.

I didn't necessarily feel *bad* about not wishing to live the American Dream, but it certainly left me questioning where my life was headed and if I'd truly be happy continuing down the road I was on.

I felt a sense of urgency after closing the final chapter to yet another book—one I'd read about two years before the 'lifestyle designers' and nomads appeared before me—Elizabeth Gilbert's *Eat, Pray, Love*.

A friend suggested I read it after she'd heard me talk about how I'd like to travel a bit someday. Having only ever been to the Canadian side of Niagara Falls once, Vancouver for a few days, and maybe a half a dozen or so states, I hadn't done much traveling in my 28 years. There was a part of me that had become tired of hearing myself talk about wanting to travel, but not actually doing anything about it.

My favorite part of the day had become walking to the Clover Food Lab Truck in Dewey Square, near South Station, during lunch breaks from my full-time job as a Communications Specialist for the World Society for the Protection of Animals (WSPA). It was my second "real-life human job" as one of my friends would say (i.e., an adult, career-focused job).

I'd almost always order the chickpea falafel with a side of rosemary fries and a blueberry lemonade. There was nothing like scooching into the shade of one of the small park trees while balancing a deliciously messy meal in one hand, and a new book about travel or entrepreneurship in the other.

After I'd finished reading a few chapters one afternoon, I suddenly felt overwhelmed by unknown possibilities. With a full belly, I lied back on the grass, and propped my head up with the orange book. Maybe the know-how would seep into my brain if I just stayed there for a while. I closed my eyes and let the still air fill my chest. I had never meditated before, but I'm pretty sure this was as close to something like mediation that I'd ever done.

Allowing my mind to slow down and focus on listening to the sounds around me—the leaves rustling in the breeze, quiet

conversations from other lunch-breakers, and sparrows' songs—
I took a deep breath in and made a quiet promise to myself
that spring: I, too, would shoot for the stars.

One afternoon following a pleasant lunch full of business
brainstorming and goal setting between myself and a pad and
pen, I returned to my cubicle and settled in for the last haul of
the day. 'Click.' Two hundred new emails since lunch. Awesome. I rolled my head and neck fully around—once to the left
and once to the right—gave a big two-arm stretch upward, and
settled my hands lightly atop the keyboard. With my left fingers
lightly resting upon A, S, D, F, and right on J, K, L, colon/
semicolon, I took a deep breath in, and as I exhaled, BAM!
"Will Travel for Vegan Food" flashed before my eyes. What?
Where? It practically shot me straight out of my chair from the
base of my heels. Electric! Suddenly I realized I had opened
a new email window and was drafting a note to my parents
outlining this crazy idea that JUST came to me—to maybe,
possibly, hopefully travel the country in search of vegan food!
   "Yes, I'll live out of my car, come up with a plan to generate
donations, and travel full-time while writing about the restaurants, and maybe even interviewing restaurant owners!" I wrote.
   A few days later, Dad replied, "Cool idea, Kris!"
   It felt like a virtual pat on the head, as if to say, "Well, isn't
that a cute idea that probably won't happen because it's too
risky and, really, who would do that anyway?"
   I'd find out later, long after the journey was well underway,
that my dad had initially believed the trip was a bad idea. He
didn't want to discourage me, but was concerned that I'd be
leaving a secure job. He thought I'd be throwing away my
career path, and that relying on donations was not sustainable.

Even though, at that point, I'd been vegan for about four
years and was, in that very moment, sitting behind a desk at a
nonprofit animal welfare organization—doing work that not

only enabled me to put my graduate degree to use, but also felt aligned with my moral and ethical beliefs—I still felt like I hadn't quite hit my 'yes, this is exactly what I should be doing with my life' stride. Then again, part of me had succumbed to the idea that *knowing* my life's purpose wasn't an actual thing. That it's something people just say in order to feel better about the whole 'why we're here' thing.

But when the words "Will Travel For Vegan Food" presented themselves to me, it was the most awake I'd ever felt about what I needed to do: help spread the word about veganism by showcasing how easy it is to travel while eating only vegan foods. I'd use my marketing and communications background to feature the restaurants I'd visit, while fulfilling my desire to travel and explore this beautiful country!

It all made so much sense, in fact, that I never once questioned whether or not it should be done. I felt a deep gut-knowing that this project was exactly what I was meant to do, and the potential that it could positively impact the lives of many, including my own, was real and true.

Unlike most of the books I read that partially inspired my journey, I didn't have a major meltdown or breakthrough or hit rock bottom to trigger my desire to leave, which made me feel even crazier than I already did about the whole thing. Mostly it was that I felt unsettled. And I wasn't just planning to leave for a week or a month, but for as long as it would take to eat at every vegan restaurant in the United States. Or maybe—as it would turn out—for as long as it would take to find *myself*.

Over-the-top excited about the prospect of such an adventure, I began talking about it so much that it seemed as though the pieces started to move in that direction almost on their own. Opportunities arose, incredible resources surfaced, and new people came into my life—all so perfectly timed to the rhythm and flawless cadence of this dance toward an adventure like nothing I'd ever before imagined.

By early spring 2011, I decided to be more deliberate about the idea of such an endeavor. I gave my notice at the WSPA and began working remotely for a vegan marketing company in their social media department. I also started my own LLC to house freelance work and upcoming projects, began teaching myself how to set up a WordPress website in order to create my first for-profit business model, and more thoroughly formulated the steps I'd need to take in order to spend a year driving, writing, and eating my way through the United States.

It was all happening quickly and, before I knew it, I was welcoming strangers from Craigslist into my apartment so they could pick up items I had posted for sale. I mailed most of my book collection off to various friends, and—in agreement with my housemates—left behind my bed, loveseat, some shelving, and the television. The few things I couldn't sell or donate were packed into boxes and stored at my parents' house in upstate New York.

I initially intended to live out of my little grape-purple Honda Civic hatchback. It was a wisp of a thing, but it served me well those few years in Boston. Unfortunately, just a couple of months before I was to set out on the journey, someone jacked my little car, stripped it, and left it sitting in front of his mom's house for the cops to find about a month later.

Perhaps everything happens for a reason though. As a result of my beloved, tiny car being left but a shell, I used the money from selling its frame to help purchase the vehicle that would later become synonymous with the Will Travel for Vegan Food project: a huge forest green G20 Chevy Sports van. She was an older gal, but was in pretty good condition. We called her Gertrude—Gerty, for short.

When Gerty and I met, it was love at first sight. I'd spent weeks scouring Craigslist for something used, in the $1,500 price range, and conceivably livable. It was down to Gerty (at the time I called her "The Green Machine") and one other van that I'd dubbed "The Red Dragon," due to its red-and-white striped sides.

Between the kind retired couple, the van's body condition, and overall good vibes, Gerty won by a landslide.*

My courtship with Nate was like nothing I'd ever experienced before. He was an intense and steady text messaging fiend. He was romantic and lust-filled, even before we'd made any physical contact. He was unique and—most notably—he was vegan. Let the angels sing! Straight, attractive, single, and age-appropriate vegan men were—err, are—a rare breed.

It felt as though we were about to embark on the ultimate vegan love story to end all vegan love stories, and my desire to make it happen blinded me nearly as much as my hidden fear of jumping into a project, a road trip, a life-altering adventure of this magnitude. I was ready and open, and on the verge of falling hard. He was passionate and pursuing me with more fervor than I'd ever known.

By the time we first met—via a local vegan meet-up group on Facebook—I had already sold or donated almost all of my belongings. I was just a few weeks away from moving out of my Somerville apartment and into my parents' house for the final preparatory departure phase. Subconsciously, I was terrified of what it meant to completely flip my life around, and to do it on my own.

"I just can't not know what might happen between us," Nate said, late one night after a Boston area Vegan Drinks event, as we sat in his car parked a block away from my apartment. He had driven me home, where I still shared a bed with Joe, my boyfriend of nearly three years—a person whose ties with me would soon be broken, not because of Nate, but because our lives had already begun moving in opposite directions.

---

*Check out video footage from when Gerty and I first met at YouTube.com/wtfveganfood.

It was one of my last nights in Boston and, as my heart swelled with the idea that this person I'd met only a few weeks prior would consider leaving his life behind just to "see what might happen between us," I looked up and saw Joe dragging the trash barrel from our driveway to the street for the morning pick-up.

The proverbial fork in the road suddenly slapped me in the face. In front of me, in the distance, my current life—once defined by a comfortable job, a comfortable apartment, and a comfortable relationship—and that of a new path filled with unknown adventure, storybook romance, and full-time travel.

There was no question; with absolutely every ounce of all I was and all I had been moving toward, the choice was epically clear.

CHAPTER 2

BRAKING

Nate walked away in a huff and sat on a bench about 20 feet from me, in Millennium Park. The three months *after* that cold, cold night in the van—back in Allston—had arrived.

We had just finished talking loudly and impatiently at each other after a failed attempt at recording the last 'dance-a-day' video.

"You can't just run out of the shot and expect me to follow you around like that!" he said.

"I didn't realize you weren't able to follow, or that it was such a big deal," I retorted.

I had been dragging Nate around Chicago for the entire month of January so that I could participate in that year's Art Clash Collective Fun-a-Day Project.

The concept was as follows: choose a new public location and song every single day, dance around to the song while wearing earbuds so no one else can hear the music, have Nate record it, and then share it on YouTube. In many ways, it was a long-winded out-of-comfort-zone challenge for us both.

We had spent the previous three months exploring the entire vegan foodie landscapes of Maine, Vermont, New Hampshire, and Illinois; as well as parts of Massachusetts, New York, and Montreal.

One of my favorite jaunts with Nate was when we spent a couple weeks in New York City the first month of the trip. It was a whirlwind! We split our stay between my friend's home in New Jersey, house-sitting while she and her husband were away, and then at Sanctuary Guest Suites in Manhattan—a beautifully tranquil B&B run by Hare Krishna. While staying at Sanctuary, we joined staff and other guests one morning in Tompkins Square Park to serve freshly made meals to those in need. They do this every Wednesday and Friday, every single week of the year.

We spent a day with Ben Strothmann, AKA the Vegan Drag Queen, Honey LaBronx. We first joined her as guests on her YouTube cooking show, and then sat down with Ben to interview him for the Will Travel... YouTube channel. We were treated to a grand tour and a number of meals by our new vegan friends Stage and Johana, enjoying meals with them at Angelica Kitchen, Caravan of Dreams, and Candle 79—squeezing in a stop at MooShoes too.

We popped over to the second floor of a classy bar to celebrate our Boston-area friend's vegan wedding reception, and indulged in sandwiches at Terri and seitan scaloppini at Blossom. We more than once gorged ourselves at Lula's Sweet Apothecary (known now as simply Blythe Anne's), and browsed the fair-trade, re-purposed, and alternative energy products at Sanctuary NYC. Nate and I nearly passed out from overpleasured taste buds after dinner at Quintessence, and went for drinks at Pine Box Rock Shop in Brooklyn before a midnight meal at Foodswings. On another night out on the town, Palá offered up a romantic candlelit pizza and gnocchi dinner.

Amid all the food and meeting and dining out with new friends, most of whom had been following the start of our journey and reached out once we'd arrived in NYC, we also celebrated the arrival of "Will Travel for Vegan Food" bumper stickers—to leave behind along with window decals—as well as the installation of a custom mattress for the van.

It was fun and exciting, but I'd be lying if I said it wasn't overshadowed by the undertone of what was or wasn't developing between us romantically. There was so much going on between planning, meeting new people, writing for the blog, editing video content, managing social media, answering email inquires, scheduling routes, and the like, that the first full five months or so of the journey felt like one giant, blurry, slow start.

Even so, we spent those months falling in and out of love, being annoyed, being neutral, being happy, being stressed out of our freakin' minds. It wasn't just the close living quarters or the fact that we hardly knew each other before agreeing to go on this journey together that led to our breaking point. The truth is, the incredible momentum we'd sparked—when we first seriously discussed his joining the trip—paired with my lack of confidence, led to the swiftest 180° emotional spin ever.

Expectations were set as quickly as they were dashed. Before we even moved into the van together, Nate's text messages went from, "the L word might be inevitable," to, "I see us more as friends who are intimate." The worst part was, aside from possibly being overly excited and engaged, I had no clue why things had shifted so drastically. I'm still not clear what it was about my personality that turned Nate off so much that he felt the need to tell me about it. And I never did bring myself to ask.

Though historically confident and expressive in work—and opinions and views on life in general—when it comes to romantic partnerships, I notoriously lose the ability to speak with openness and convey how I'm feeling. My best guess is that it's due to fearing how my love interest will react—more specifically that they'd be put off and want out.

But, by the time I was willing to admit that something was off, I already felt emotionally tied to the idea that I'd no longer have to go on the trip by myself. And I held on to the thought that maybe we'd grow into a fairytale romance after all. We just needed a little more time. Just a little more.

It didn't help that we could never get away, or recoup, or center ourselves. There was never a break. I'd find myself locked in public restrooms whisper-sobbing on the phone to my mom. "I just can't do this anymore," I'd say, reciting that week's pain points, hurtful conversations, and confusion about how we had gone from sweet courting to cold chaos, in a matter of weeks.

To be fair, I *was* warned ahead of time. A few weeks before he joined me on the trip, I befriended Samantha, one of Nate's closest friends, and took refuge in her words of encouragement; or, in some cases, discouragement. There was a conversation she and I had just one week before I was set to pick Nate up and welcome him as an official member of the Will Travel for Vegan Food team. I shared with her my shock and sadness at his sudden decision to just be "friends who are intimate," as it was explained to me.

Though I tried to play it off as cool in that conversation with him, in actuality I was utterly crushed. I told him I was fine with it, that we'd work things out, and that I had no expectations, all while thinking, 'how is this possible, what if it doesn't work out, I thought we were going to fall in love big time.'

Samantha advised me to tell him how I felt, and suggested I not bring him along for the journey after all.

"I know him too well," she said. "I think he might still have feelings for his ex; and besides, based on what you're saying HE said, it just sounds like a recipe for disaster."

Her words set heavy. So heavy. I knew she was right though. But I also knew I couldn't bring myself to change our plan. He had already made arrangements to leave his Allston apartment, and we had celebrated the success of our journey's beginning. It was already set in motion and I was well on my way to the continuation of my fear-avoidance dating pattern of back-to-back relationships.

I slammed on the brakes, and swerved hard to the left into the middle turning lane—everything in the van whooshed forward in slow motion with the momentum.

With a loud crash and metal bang, we collided hard. Gerty's right front tire made a loud, winded 'pop' as I continued pedaling the brake to slow us down, a burnt rubber smell now filling the air. When Gerty finally came to a halt, the seatbelt was uncomfortably tight across my chest, and my hands were sore and sweaty from gripping the steering wheel with all my might.

I exhaled slowly—I must have been holding my breath—and then looked through the rearview mirror to see the other car's front end completely separated from its body, laying in the middle of the road a few feet behind me. 'Oh my god, oh my god, oh my god,' I thought. 'I hope whoever is in that car is okay.'

The strange thing is that I recall this very scene flashing before my eyes, seconds before it happened, and yet I wasn't able to avoid smashing into the 93-year-old man's vehicle. He had pulled out of the Off Track Betting (OTB) parking lot on Route 22, in New Lebanon, New York; and stopped in oncoming traffic.

Moments after realizing that I was okay, though stunned and shaking, I hopped out of the van and jogged to the elderly man's car. A few people had already begun circling, and some of his friends from OTB were squatting next to the open driver's side door, talking to him. He was shaken up, but okay.

Some time later, a couple police officers took our individual statements. I called AAA, who sent someone to replace Gerty's blown tire, and assessed that she seemed fine otherwise.

Though, from then on, her steering wheel would always settle slightly to the left, while driving straight ahead.

As cheesy as it sounds, I can't help but think the accident was a sign. From whom, I don't know. But I had been on my way to Boston to pick up Nate so we could officially start the trip together. They/it tried to warn me earlier with Nate's changed behavior, and with the uncertainty I felt inside; and then again with Samantha telling me outright that she believed I shouldn't take him with me at all. But I didn't listen. And I hadn't listened on this day either. Once Gerty's tire was repaired, I continued on as if nothing had happened.

Part of me thought it was silly to even *think* it was anything remotely close to a sign. Accidents happen all the time; why was this one any different? Then again, I had never been in one before. And I haven't been in one since.

But, back to Chicago.

I glanced over my right shoulder at the Cloud Gate sculpture, wishing it were the spaceship I wanted it to be. I imagined walking up to its silver, reflective exterior, holding an arm out and being blooped into the structure, to join David and the Puckmarin on a grand adventure.

It felt as though an eternity was passing as everything around me seemed to be frozen in time, while I stood, at my wit's end, nearly hyperventilating from the constant emotional duo that had been tailing me for months now: anxiety and exhaustion. And from the pain, sorrow, and confusion that encompassed a journey that was *supposed* to be fun and magical. Not one that had me afraid to speak up for myself, afraid that this daily sick-to-my-stomach feeling had become the norm, and afraid of love. Period.

I looked back at Nate sitting on the bench. He was facing away from the park's center and I, with my shoulders square

to him, closed my eyes. Words spoken by my new yogi friend
Ryan came to me: "The next time you feel powerless, or hurt,
or lost, say to him in your mind: 'I recall my energy back to
me. And I return your energy back to you.' Visualize it and
believe it. Whatever he has going on need not be yours. And
yours need not be his."

I took a huge breath in, "I recall my energy back to me.
And I return your energy back to you." And let a deep breath
out, "I recall my energy back to me. And I return your energy
back to you."

This would mark the first time in the history of my life that
I believed—out of desperation for some form of relief—in the
power of mind over matter. Of energy. Of intention.

I repeated this with each breath, three times, and then released
the pattern. Before opening my eyes, I silently added a final note:
"I'm closing the door on this now."

When I opened my eyes, I was surprised to see Nate standing
in front of me. "Hey," he said, "I'm sorry about that misun-
derstanding. Do you want to go film the video on one of the
train platforms?"

"Hey, thanks. Sure. Yeah, that sounds good," I said.

Nate tapped away on his phone in search of the nearest L
station as we walked up North Michigan Avenue in a renewed,
comfortable silence.

I couldn't help but give a silent thank-you to whomever, or
whatever, helped me through that moment. Something in me
changed. An understanding and openness occurred that felt
new. And with that came the very clear realization that I had
intended to go on this van-dwelling excursion by myself. So,
what was I doing with this person? What was I doing with
someone I hardly knew? What kind of pressures had I inad-
vertently placed on him and myself? Perhaps whatever I had
been creating—out of that fear of being alone emotionally and
physically, out of drastically changing my life, out of letting

go of a potentially game-changing love story—is what Nate was picking up, and *that* kept us at odds and out of romance.

I had only myself to point at. And it was time to make a change. One that would redirect the course of the road trip, my relationship with Nate, and my relationship with myself.

CHAPTER 3

AS IT WAS INTENDED

"The risk of a wrong decision is
preferable to the terror of indecision."

MAIMONIDES

There was a calm in the air between us as we headed back to Massachusetts from Illinois. Though we hadn't yet talked about him leaving the trip, I knew that it had to be so. There was a part of me that felt he sensed it too.

It was the first week of February, about five months into the trip, and we were on our way back to Boston—yet again. We'd made a version of this trip a half a dozen times or so since beginning the journey, due to various previously made commitments and whatnot. This time it was for a snowboarding trip that Nate had planned with some friends.

As we backtracked over Indiana, Ohio, and Pennsylvania, I longed for our time apart. I worried about how the 'it's time I go it alone' conversation would shake out, once he returned from the snowboarding trip, and fantasized about momentarily running away from it all by way of someone else's embrace.

Anyone, really.

As the miles between the Chicago suburbs and Gerty's bumper grew farther apart, I began to recall the pre-road trip trial we faced in Maine, back in August.

———

Still riding the high of our new discovery of one another, we thought it'd be fun to spend a few days in Maine together, while checking that state off of our to-visit list.

We dined at all six of the state's vegan restaurants that week—my favorites being Eden Vegetarian Café in Bar Harbor and The Green Elephant in Portland—spent a few nights at my friend Jeanette's place, and camped out when we got farther north. Nate and I attended a local vegetarian potluck where we gave our first-ever impromptu speeches about the trip, our goals, and what was next.

It would be the first time we'd be in each other's company without any moral restrictions. And it would mark the first notable blip in the steady decline of our short-lived venture together.

From the start of this pre-road trip trial period, I began with my signature awkward, shy, and nervous routine. I only ever got this way around someone I really, really liked. And, since we would now have the opportunity to fully express ourselves and be close, I felt the pressure to 'show up,' and be cool and sexy and fun and anything that would make me desirable to Nate.

After a few PG nights on Jeanette's couch, some street-side handholding, and in-restaurant shoulder bumping, we were alone at last. In a tent. Next to the world's loudest family—and their toddler—at the first KOA campground we'd spotted.

Setting up the tent was fun. We made vegan s'mores that night, our smiles turned red with wine-soaked lips, and we giggled and shyly flirted the first night away.

By the close of day two of our northern Maine adventure, my sense of insecurity set in after witnessing what I believed to be shared interest between Nate and another vegan gal at the earlier potluck we had attended. I tried to shake it off, but I'm about as good at hiding my feelings as Bruce Banner is. Instead of voicing any concerns, I withdrew. Because that's what I do. And instead of prying, Nate focused on external annoyances like the midnight screaming toddler at the campsite next door.

It was our last night together before the trial period ended, before I returned to my folks' place in upstate New York and he returned to Boston for more trip planning, organizing, and fundraising. So, I initiated what turned into an awkward and snooze-worthy intimate encounter.

"Nate," I whispered, leaning in for a kiss. He was lying on his back, facing the roof of the tent, and I was curled up next to him, on my right side. He didn't lean into the kiss, but let me place one on the corner of his mouth. I paused, expecting him to turn toward me or to kiss me back. But there was nothing.

I rested my head back down on the pillow overtop Nate's outstretched arm, contemplating another move.

"Ahh. That kid is so annoying!" Nate whispered back.

"Yeah," I said.

I placed my left hand on Nate's chest and slowly began moving it down, across his stomach, and then lower. As I started unbuttoning his pants, I looked back toward him. He was still staring straight up at the roof.

I wasn't sure if he wasn't into it, and wondered if I should stop. Or if maybe I should be trying harder to get his attention. Did he enjoy what I was doing? Did he find pleasure in not reacting? What was he waiting for? He was silent and motionless. But it was our last night together for a while and I wanted him to know that I was attracted to him, and cared for him, and wanted to kick things up a notch. So, I climbed on top of him and began kissing him more passionately. I ran my hands through his thick beard and pressed my hips against his.

He started kissing me back, and running his hands along my sides. But there was something devastatingly flat about the whole thing. The passion was at zero knots, and his touch felt uninspired.

With Nate focused on the annoying neighbor, and me uncomfortably trying to regain his attention so we could spend our last night together in sexy-time bliss, it basically left us both wondering what the hell we were in for.

In light of my yet-to-be-realized 'afraid to be on my own but can't see it' dating pattern, as soon as my relationship's walls began breaking down, I was subconsciously on the hunt for someone else to cling to, to make me feel wanted and not alone.

While Nate was snowboarding, I knelt to pick up the pieces of my broken heart and placed them in the hands of another man. I holed up, curled into the arms, into the love, and into the heat of this man—as captivating as King Leonidas himself.

We'd met through mutual friends, via Facebook, a few months earlier. Conversations had been intermittent and mildly flirty on occasion. The further apart Nate and I had grown over the past few months, the more frequently I'd been chatting and growing closer to Leonidas. We'd never actually met in person before then.

It wasn't much, but it didn't need to be. I had been craving emotional escape for more than five months by that point. This gentle man made me feel more important and more cared for in our few days together than I had felt ever before, single or with anyone else.

What set this brief rendezvous so far apart from anything I'd experienced previously was the fact that we did not talk of dating or being together. We did not talk of what was to come next or what we'd leave behind. Unlike all of my previous romantic encounters—where my first concern was 'where is this going,' or 'will it last'—I could, for the first time in my dating life, just be. Just be next to him. Just be near him. Just be me. Out of my head and into the moment.

We spent days wrapped in blankets, building forts, watching sci-fi movies, drinking wine, and eating all the frozen vegan pizza pies we could find. We ate ice cream until we got sick, set world records for most snuggles had in a day, and laughed about absolutely nothing.

With every hour we spent together, my approach and outlook on romance was being redefined in nearly every way. Even though I wouldn't recognize it until many months later, I was officially shedding a layer of unhealthy, expectation-driven relationship habits.

Breathe.

I took a sip of my ginger root beer and set the bottle gently down onto the metal tabletop. After clearing my throat and taking a tempered breath in, I said, "I think I'm ready to go it alone now."

Nate had returned from his snowboarding excursion. We were sitting next to one another at Peace O' Pie, in Allston, Massachusetts, just a few blocks away from where we had been parked on that cold, cold night six months earlier.

My eyes began to well, but before I had time to enter full body sweat, panic mode, Nate replied evenly, "Okay. What made you decide that?"

"Well," I began, "as you know, I initially intended to do this thing by myself. And, it seems like we're both just really struggling, trying to do it together."

I looked down at my balled up hands in my lap, then caught Nate's glance before quickly looking away again.

"Okay," he said. "I think I understand. But. It's just. It's tough, ya know? I gave up a career, housing, and a whole life here, to go on the trip."

"I know. I'm so sorry," I said, keeping my eyes down. "But, please know that I'm so grateful for all you did to help get everything going. If it weren't for you, I don't know if I would have ever gotten started."

It was true. Nate had taken the lead on many of the early tasks within trip planning, including researching, designing, and ordering the bumper stickers, window decals, and project-themed t-shirts. He used his audio engineering background to improve the quality of our video interviews, revamped the inside of the van to make it livable, contributed dozens of blog posts, and did 99% of the driving.

Nate reached over and squeezed my hands. I looked up and met his eyes, and we both smiled a little.

As my mom has always said, "everyone comes into your life for a reason." And perhaps Nate's purpose was to help me not only get going and officially set out on the journey, but also to begin my process of learning how to let go, and to be on my own. To make independent decisions, and to learn the great value that comes from a little self-love.

The time passed quickly, but we talked openly for hours over our slices of gourmet vegan pizza, breadsticks, and Zevia sodas. Somehow we seemed warmer toward each other, and more understanding than we'd been in months. With the expectation of a relationship dropped, a friendship remained.

We agreed to part ways. Nate would take the next few weeks to find housing and move his belongings out of the van, while I would catch up on writing for the blog, and spend time with some of my closest friends, and my King Leonidas.

Nate and I would part as friends who loved and supported one another, and wished each other well.

For the time being, anyway.

"I love you," I said, slapping a hand over my mouth in shock. I'd never before uttered those words to someone without it being fully thought out and intentional. Or, in a couple of cases, saying it in return so the other person wouldn't feel bad. But now, they slipped out more naturally than perhaps ever before in my life.

I think I looked more surprised than my Leonidas did. I felt compelled to march away in embarrassment, but he pulled me in and hugged the awkward away. I softened and turned beet red.

We walked, arms around each other's waists, out to the van, now lighter in both weight and energy.

The King added a few patches to the van's leaky corners and backed her out of the narrow, car-lined driveway for me. We hugged once more before I climbed up into the driver's seat. I think we knew we'd never see each other again, and we were both okay with it. For the first time, I was okay with it.

I don't know, maybe I did fall in love with my Leonidas. But it was for very different reasons than I'd ever loved anyone else. Without effort, he took away pain, introduced ease, and helped me begin to scrape away a very deep-seated layer of a part of myself that needed to evolve. He did this unknowingly though. He did this simply by being himself, which is perhaps why maybe I did love him after all.

The air was brisk and the sun was shining brightly that winter morning as I pulled onto Interstate 95 North. An enormous sense of calm and silence washed over my core. Then came vibrant elation as I realized that, for the first time in six months, I could belt aloud to whatever came on the radio!

I twisted the radio dial clockwise, and then the volume button too, and there it was: "Hold On" by Wilson freakin' Phillips. I turned the volume button another 180°, rolled down the passenger side window—because the driver's side window wasn't working and it was kind of cold anyway—and my heart lifted.

My hands bounced off the steering wheel and I shout-sang along with Carnie, Wendy, and Chynna until tears rolled off my cheeks in existential joy, release, and recognition of the present moment.

"YOU GOT YOURSELF INTO YOUR OWN MESS... DON'T YOU THINK IT'S WORTH YOUR TIME TO CHANGE YOUR MIND? ...hold on for one more day."

CHAPTER 4

BY CHANCE

"Can I get you anything else, my dear?" the young waitress repeated; her arms beautifully decorated with colorful ink featuring various pieces and styles of art.

I momentarily broke my trance and looked up at her. "Oh. No, I think that'll do it. Thank you," I said. I smiled before she turned to walk away.

I was staring in a daze, down at "The Veganator Scramble" — a large, bright blue plate muted by sautéed tofu, mushrooms, peppers, onions, broccoli, and spices, topped with hot sauce, tucked against a side of salty steak fries.

I chose this dish primarily because of its name. *Terminator* is one of my many favorite movies of all time. Well, *T2* that is. The onions and peppers were still quietly hissing, scorched from the grill. The afternoon sunlight shone in through the big corner window seat at the front of the restaurant, breaking through the airy waves of steam that rose from the tippy top of the scramble heap.

It was late February and I was dining by myself at Silly's Restaurant in Portland, Maine. I would soon grow accustomed to dining out by myself, as it would become one of the very things that defined a facet of my lifestyle for at least the subsequent 18 months. But something extraordinary was about to happen, as I remained locked on to that plate of food.

Without reason, my heartbeat quickened and, feeling almost removed from my body, I watched in what seemed like microscopic slow motion as the hair on my arms lifted, an extension of the cold chills that were setting in. Tucked into the near corner of the window seat, I placed my right hand on my chest and the other, palm flat on the table to steady myself.

I looked over my left shoulder, vision blurred and surrounding sounds sharpened. Utensils clanked out of synch, against plates and one another. The conversations from the tables of twos and fours seemed to get louder and more piercing. And then, WHOOSH!

Silence.

Suddenly all was still. Frozen. Like the moment Brody witnessed his first shark attack off the coast of Amity, the would-be cameraman performing a perfectly orchestrated Zolly, rapidly zooming in to the expression on my face, the background retreating and turning into a twisty, vertigo version of itself.

And in the stillness came a knowing as clear as if someone were sitting right beside me, speaking the words softly into my ear:

"Kristin, do you see where you are? In the very same seat, of the very same restaurant, inside the very same city, of the very same state wherein you shared your first road trip meal with Nate. You intended to make this journey a solo mission. And when you tried to loop in another—out of fear of the unknown, out of fear of being alone—you experienced pain, anguish, and pushback. You've now been sent back to 'GO.' It is time to begin again, by yourself this time, just as you originally intended. Ready, set, ..." INHALE!

With a gigantic breath, my chest heaved forward.

And there I was. Back in the present moment. Mouth agape, one hand still over my chest. I lifted my other hand from the table, leaving behind a sweaty imprint that immediately began to disappear, removing all traces of my fleeting, out-of-body flash in time.

It was remarkably clear now—all the rush, the confusion, the anguish, the unsteadiness of it all. Though my deep desire to embark on this journey did lead me to actionable, forward-moving steps, it was my fear that had held me back from experiencing what I was meant to.

It was as if someone plucked me up by the scruff of my shoulders and gently carried me back in time. To begin again. Not just to begin again anywhere, but in the exact same place where it had begun. Ready or not, it's round two. Ding! Ding! Ding!

I looked down at my plate of food and it, too, had calmed. No more hiss or rising heat. And I knew, in that moment, there were only four things left to do: pick up my phone, take a picture of my meal, post it to Instagram and Facebook and Twitter, and then eat.

I wasn't terribly hungry, but needed to kill some time before meeting up with my friend Jeanette, who I came to know years earlier while interning with the New England Anti-Vivisection Society (NEAVS), where she worked as their program and administrative assistant. She was teaching a yoga class downtown and then had a business meeting regarding the opening of her first brick-and-mortar business: Roost House of Juice.

It was Jeanette who had suggested I read *Eat, Pray, Love* those few years ago. And it was the NEAVS crew—made up of no more than four or five vegan women at the time—who would become my mentors, closest Boston area friends, and some of the biggest supporters of this project, long before it began.

At the suggestion of Karen, one of the 'NEAVS ladies,' we formed a monthly in-person meet-up for female entrepreneurs to talk business and life, support each other in our dreams, and celebrate our achievements. I'd get so fired up in those meetings. In a good way. I'd always come away inspired, full of ideas, and feeling more creative than ever. They became the highlight of every month! And, with each meeting, I could feel deep within, that I was drawing closer to something big. Something important. Something life-changing. But I had no idea it would be quite like this.

I hadn't been back to Maine since that awkward camping excursion Nate and I had taken six months earlier. It was doubly exciting this time. Not only was I given a chance to hit the reset button on the personal side of the journey, and visit with Jeanette, but I was also about to meet, for the first time in-person, my yogi friend Ryan, who had most helped me through the difficulties with Nate. At this point, he'd become more of a close, spiritual guru, in a way.

After discovering the dance-a-day videos in January, by way of Jeanette sharing a few on her Facebook page, Ryan reached out to me:

"I just messaged Jeanette to this end, but your videos really are delightful and inspiring! I laughed out loud, clapped my hands and smiled as if I were sharing the experience first-hand. On paper it's a small thing, but in essence is massive and truly brilliant! Thanks so much for sharing these videos. What a fantastic, light-hearted example and expression of joy! We all should incorporate that level of freedom and beauty into every day. So many wonderful things to learn from so many people! Thanks for being one of them."

We began emailing almost daily. I'd vent about my day's troubles, and Ryan would inevitably come back with profound statements and inquiries that led me to think about my actions, reactions, and purpose—and the lives of those around me—in ways I'd never considered, or had ever been open to before.

"I feel like you're caught in a fairly typical trap for young women today. Sex and attention from a man equates to feeling loved and self-worth. Your challenge is to identify the tendency, break the pattern, and work with the underlying fears and insecurities that fuel the pattern that is clearly not serving you," Ryan wrote once.

This is one of my favorite excerpts from an email exchange we had about my feeling overwhelmed by the situation with Nate, creating projects and working from the road, managing everything involved with making Will Travel... work, and the like:

> In general, you are doing something that I know all too well. You are dispersing your energies into so many things, so many irons in the fire, that you have constructed a life with no space to simply 'be' or to regularly and freely reflect on your own happiness and state of mind. It is a pattern that is self-reinforcing and can go on indefinitely. This is the sort of dynamic that makes it easy to tolerate a toxic relationship, to regularly be less-than-happy, generally overlook ongoing patterns that you'd prefer to break, and is steady fuel for an unstable rollercoaster effect.
>
> All this means is that 'you're over-drafting your wellness account' and the sooner you can strike a balance, the better your health and everything will be. If the over-draft runs too high, it generally leads to illness, and sometimes serious illness.
>
> Just picture your life for a moment as a giant hurricane. With all these intentions, bright ideas, obligations, struggles, emotional wounds, scattered senses of identity, and all everything else actively present in your life swirling around you. The hurricane has enough energy to continually pick up new ideas and conflicts such that you never can experience peace or glean any reasonable

sense of self. It is up to you to step into the eye, begin to know yourself, and then head back in to diffuse it, only once you have a higher sense of yourself and your most essential needs. There can be no clarity and only little bits of growth when always stuck in the swirling chaotic vortex of everything at once. Your most valuable and precious resource is you, and therefore, your wellness.

Muster up your strength, laugh in the face of fear, and know that you can change these things that repeatedly bring you unhappiness and discontentment. When beauty comes knocking, it need not be an illusion. We can create anything and everything we want and need. We just need a little more practice and to be a little less of a servant to fear.

Through Ryan's support, kind and thought-provoking words, and openness, I was able to move through one of the most difficult periods of my life in a cathartic and educational way. I owe Ryan more thanks than I could possibly communicate in a lifetime for what he's given me—this new outlook on life.

Ryan came into my life at a point when I didn't know which direction to turn or how to handle it all emotionally, while feeling that I needed to outwardly project positivity, joy, and strength to the online community that was slowly growing around the project. I often revel at how perfectly timed it was—his showing up at my proverbial doorstop. But to that, I know Ryan would simply say, "Kristin, my friend, trust in divine timing and know that absolutely nothing is by chance."

part two

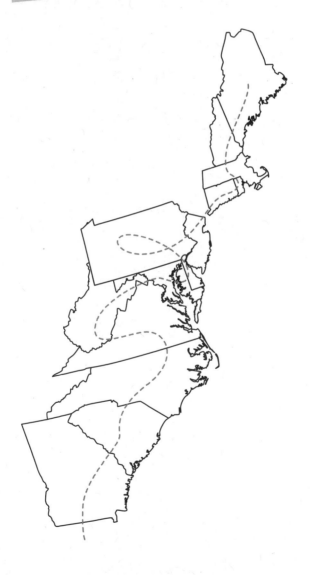

CHAPTER 5

TOGETHER WE GROW

I was home from college for another winter break, walked cautiously into my parents' living room, and flopped onto the couch as Dad stood fiddling with the TV.

Mom and Dad had been vegan for at least a year now, and I'd grown accustomed to the "Oh how'd that get on the tube" approach. Dad had taken to not so subtly introducing me to the hidden horrors of factory farming, by way of undercover footage taken by Mercy for Animals, or one of the other organizations attempting to shine light on the slaughter industry.

Cody sat up from his dog bed and carefully moseyed over to me, in his signature senior style—achy hip dysplasia and all—and rested his stout, golden muzzle, now laced with individual grey strands of fur, onto my lap.

"MOOOOOO," belted from the speakers. I looked up at the TV to a bright red, perfectly formed, thick stream of blood shooting vertically into the air from the base of a young bovine's head, who'd just had one of his horns clipped off, flush to the base of his skull.

"Dad!" I yelled. He had already casually left the room, and the burning acidic contents of my stomach began to rise. Feeling nauseated, I dropped my head, cupped my face in my hands, and lunged forward at the waist, nearly clocking heads with Cody. "Dad, stop it! Turn it off!" I shouted louder each time. "You know I can't take that stuff. Turn it off!"

"Okay, okay!" he said sheepishly, and shuffled back into the living room.

I slowly uncovered my face to reveal Cody there, his chin still on my lap. He hadn't heard a thing. I scratched his noggin behind one ear until my stomach calmed. He twisted and lifted his head into my hand; my thighs were now dotted with dog slobber. I stood and met Mom in the kitchen where she was at the sink, washing dishes.

"Ugh. Why does Dad do that?" I said. "You guys know that stuff makes me sick."

I opened the freezer door to grab the usual stash of ice cream that Dad and I would devour while we stayed up late watching sci-fi movies, until we were both snoring on opposite couches.

"So Delicious Dairy Free Chocolate Peanut Butter?" I queried, closing the door firmly. "What the heck, Mom?"

"Dad and I are trying out some new ice creams that don't have milk in them. It's good! You should give it a try," she said. I pivoted sharply on my heels and marched out of the kitchen, through the dining room, and up the stairs to my bedroom. Tigger—the first kitty to join our family when we moved into this 1950s farmhouse 10 years earlier—trotted behind me before racing up the stairs to greet me at the top.

———

In an effort to find evidence condemning a vegetarian diet, my parents took to the internet posthaste. It was the late 90s and my brother, Josh, had just returned from touring with Phish. And by touring, I mean he and some friends followed the band around for a few months during one of their US tours, selling bottles of water at the shows to make enough money to eat and likely do other things.

Upon his return home, he had a full head of knotty dreads, a handful of new tattoos, and declared his vegetarianism to my parents. Even though he wasn't living at home anymore, my parents naturally felt obligated to share their concerns with him about his lifestyle choices.

Despite their original intentions, during their investigation into a vegetarian diet, they found nothing but reports on how good it is for overall health.

After a bit of resistance followed by a few heartfelt conversations with my brother, and eye-opening documentaries on the mistreatment of animals, the negative impacts the meat industry has on the planet, and how vegetarianism relates to personal health; it didn't take much more before my parents welcomed the idea of becoming vegetarian themselves.

"We'd like to try to become vegetarian together, as a family," Mom said one afternoon. She and Dad had sat me down at the kitchen table to have the talk. Not about boys or life, but about what we were eating. It was 1999 and I was 16.

"We'll still buy you meat and keep it in the house, if you'd like. But Dad and I are going to stop eating it for a while," said Mom.

"Nah, that's okay. I guess I'll give it a try too," I replied. I've always been pretty close with my parents and have in most cases trusted their judgment.

Unlike my parents, I didn't do much initial research on the topic. All I knew was, from that point forward, I'd call myself a vegetarian. It took a year or so before my classmates stopped pestering me about it. "It's not like I'm doing it to save a cow," I'd say, feeling the pressure to come up with something nonchalant and cool. "I'm doing it because it's healthy."

My school was very small. I attended kindergarten through senior year all in the same building—gradually moving from one end of the rectangular building to the other, by way of grade level. And there were fewer than 100 graduates in my class, including one of the sons of a dairy farmer whose pastures lined the border to the grassy playground behind the school. Over the years, there were many outdoor gym and study breaks that included stretching my body over the fence to pet one of the black-and-white cows. They never did get close enough.

During senior year, Hoosick Falls Central School students were tasked with writing in-depth research papers on a topic of their choice. I chose vegetarianism. I don't remember much about that paper other than its contents affirming my resolve to remain vegetarian as I headed off to college that fall.

While I was away, studying farm management and the anatomy, physiology, biology, and healthcare of horses—in Cazenovia College's Equine Business Management program—my parents were making radical life changes. They became super involved with the area co-op, started a vegetarian meet-up group, and even began planning the first of what would become an annual vegetarian—now vegan—conference held in Albany, New York, just an hour or so from the little town I grew up in.

"Kris, you wouldn't believe this Vegetarian Summerfest event," Dad said over the phone, during one of my calls home. "It's in Pennsylvania and is one of the longest-running vegetarian conferences in the country. They have speakers from all over the world come in and talk about diet, animal welfare, and how these things impact the planet. Mom and I had a blast and plan to go back again next year!"

My parents were not only attending every vegetarian conference they could drive or bus to, but they had also become 'those' vegetarians. The ones who talked about it at every turn, gifted family members books about the topic, and spent any extra time they found in a day working toward spreading the word about all they'd learned. Thank you, Facebook.

It wasn't long before the bumper of their Subaru hatchback was decorated with multiple "go veg" stickers and animal rights declarations. As they continued to learn more about not only the meat industry, but also the dairy and egg industries—and their equally horrific practices and planetary impacts—my parents eventually became vegan.

Shortly thereafter, my Christmas presents went from shopping center gift cards and CDs of my favorite musicians, to "VEGAN" embossed hoodies, t-shirts, and stickers; and books written by Dr. T. Colin Campbell, Dr. Caldwell Esselstyn, and former cattle rancher Howard Lyman.

The open dirt floor of the barn-like building was interrupted periodically by rustic, structural beams posted every few feet down the center, creating pseudo aisles where rows and rows of vintage folding chairs sat facing the north wall. Part of me expected a bluegrass hoedown to break out at any moment— right there in Syracuse, New York's Inner Harbor. Well, any dancing would do in place of the inevitably dry and boring talk I was preparing to sit in on.

"Why Dairy Isn't Necessary," read the program, as the title of Registered Dietitian George Eisman's lecture.

I carefully selected one of the seats toward the back of the room. Its slats creaked under the pressure of my weight, and I held my breath, sitting picture still for a second or two, until the chair seemed to settle and we agreed together that it could hold me.

I watched in judgment as people of all ages piled in, chatting with one another about herbs, essential oils, and organic food shares. It was August 27th, 2006 and I was 24 years old.

George Eisman emerged from a small swarm of fans, and took to the platform in front of the now full rows of chairs. He began talking as I continued to look around the room, taking stock of the organic hemp reusable bags, Klean Kanteen water bottles, Birkenstock sandals, and the scent of patchouli oil filling the air. Actually, that's a lie. I don't recall smelling patchouli oil at all, but there was a part of me that expected to—wanted to, even. Just to confirm my blanketed suspicion of hippy-dom.

It wasn't my typical nature to observe others on such a critical scale, but I clearly felt apprehensive about all the vegetarians and vegans bustling around me. Even though I had been eating strictly vegetarian for eight years by that point, I still believed that veganism was taking it too far and that all those people around me were likely crazy.

But then my ears caught something: "The idea that human beings need the milk of another species is ludicrous, and the idea that any animals need milk beyond infancy makes no scientific sense at all…" Mr. Eisman said.

Suddenly I was sharply focused on his words, and the dozens of people I had been spending time stereotyping, those sitting all around me engrossed in the lecture, began to fade away.

He continued, "Milk is a secretion for growth intended for an animal that's meant to grow hundreds of pounds larger than us. And making an animal into a dairy cow in this country is the worst thing we can imagine doing to any animal…"

I was locked in now. I couldn't hear or see anything or anyone else other than George Eisman. The entire barn might as well have gone dark, but a single spotlight hovering over me in my unstable chair—like that epic scene from *Fire in the Sky*—the echo of his words ringing in sync with my heartbeat. In that moment, everything changed. I finally heard loud and clear all the surrounding chatter I'd been pushing away for the past couple years, from my parents and their vegan friends.

I walked out of the barn and into the bright afternoon sun that shone over the waterfront. I rubbed my eyes to clear away the haze, and spotted my parents and their small clan of elite Albany vegans. Dawn was making friends with a hedgehog curled up in the hood of its caregivers sweatshirt, and my parents were in a deep conversation with Olga and Jim about dreams of starting their own food- and education-oriented veggie festival down in Albany or Troy.

After saying goodbye to my folks, Lyle—my then-boyfriend of three years—and I headed back to my little white Plymouth Acclaim. I dropped Lyle off at work, swung by the nearest Pizza Hut, and picked up a personal pan pizza with a side of breadsticks. I drove to our place in High Acres Apartments, just off of Ball Road, and settled in while watching that season's *Dancing with The Stars* lineup of celebrities and their professional instructor pairings.

I looked over at Fenny—my Creamsicle-colored, longhaired, small coon kitty, that I'd adopted one year earlier from a rescue in Shaftsbury, Vermont—and then looked down at my little veggie supreme. I made an agreement with myself just then: this would be my last non-vegan meal, ever.

CHAPTER 6

ALONE

It had been about one month since Nate's departure from the trip, and I had since meandered my way through the remaining vegan eateries in Massachusetts, Rhode Island, and Connecticut, before arriving in Philadelphia.

While carefully inching the van's 17-foot-long frame forward then backward, forward then backward, into an epically small parallel parking space in the jammed streets of South Philly, it occurred to me that since Nate's absence, this was the first time I had truly been completely on my own, ever in my life. And single too, for that matter. Well, since the age of 16.

I've had a total of three "big" or truly deep and meaningful romantic relationships in my life to-date—you know, the ones that feel huge and typically change you in some small or big way—with a handful of those 'a few months here, a few months there' type of relationships before and between the substantial ones.

First, there was Ed. Tall, sweet, and incredibly thoughtful. We went to the same high school, but didn't connect romantically until the summer before we shipped off to college. I was in Cazenovia and he was in Rochester. We were on again off again (but mostly on) during our first three years of college, until I met Lyle through a mutual friend.

Despite a somewhat slow and cautious start—and as my relationship with Ed fizzled out—Lyle and I hit our romantic stride; there was no question we were both in it, full on.

I remember lying in bed with him one afternoon. He still lived with his parents, but they were at work on this day. The house was peacefully quiet and we were wrapped in each other's arms, legs intertwined so crazily that I thought we'd be unable to unfurl. There's no way we could get physically closer than we were at that moment—our bodies pressed so tightly against the other, it was almost painful—and yet it still wasn't close enough. I shut my eyes and pictured our physical bodies turning into sparkly, floating particles that would dance around and within each other's until we were indistinguishable from one another.

Lyle and I were together during my last year of college and for two years after that. We spent one year doing the long distance thing—while I lived in Plymouth, Massachusetts, working at my first real job out of college—and one year living together in Syracuse, where I moved to be with him, and to participate in an internship at Syracuse.com in an effort to build up marketing credentials, as I planned to apply to graduate schools. It would mark the first time in my life that I shared living space with a boyfriend.

Our long distance relationship wasn't easy, and I thought living together would heal all wounds we'd created while apart. But, by the time I had learned of my acceptance into Emerson College's Integrated Marketing Communication (IMC) graduate program, Lyle had decided he wanted to stay in Syracuse, and we both decided long distance wasn't what either of us wanted.

Of course, these are simplifications of the young and emotionally-driven relationships I had with both guys. I was only just beginning to uncover my fear-based pattern of always feeling like I needed to be with someone, realizing how inattentive and careless I was with sweet Ed, and how ill-matched a couple Lyle and I truly were, once the particle lust phase had run its course. Something else had begun to emerge from reflection on those relationships too—that they had each lasted at least one year too long, and there was little if any downtime between them.

It'd be another year, encompassed with three or four mini, un-blossomed relationships, before I'd meet Joe.

It was a sunny and finally warm summer afternoon out on the Boston Common. Just coming off our first year of grad school—benchmarking the halfway point of the program— my closest IMC classmates were engaged in a pick-up game of soccer with some of the crew from the Writing, Literature, and Publishing (WLP) program.

My dear friend Hisham and I sat on the sidelines, soaking up the rays as my eyes followed our fellow classmates and the soccer ball, bouncing from one side of the makeshift field to the other. As our friend Melis knelt to retrieve the ball, my gaze landed just beyond her to the shade of a nearby tree where a dashingly stocky, bearded fellow with thin, wiry glasses sat, book in hand.

I squinted for a better look and nudged Hisham. "Who is THAT?" I asked.

He shrugged and said, "Must be one of the new WLP'ers." Hisham extended his camera out at arm's length, pulled me in and said, "NONDAIRY CHEEEEEESE!"

The shutter snapped, and just as the photo captured that moment in time, so too has my memory held onto that day I first saw Joe.

He was just a couple inches taller than I was and effortlessly stocky. Seriously, I don't know how infrequent, if any, exercise equals crazy muscle mass, but he was somehow forever muscle-y. He also possessed my personal favorite combo: brunette, bearded, and tattooed. Throw in a cute button nose; dial up those baby browns; excuse the stubbornness, occasional cockiness, and conflicting dietary preferences; and Joe was—for all intents and purposes—my perfect ten.

I could have called it though. The estimated countdown to the close of our relationship. If not for the simple fact that most relationships end at *some* point anyway, but based primarily on the practically tangible two- to three-year timeline that seemed to dictate the duration of every long-term romance I ever had.

Three apartments and two and a half years later, I decided to leave. To leave Boston, to leave my job, to leave our Somerville apartment, and to leave a great number of things that were going well.

"Well, you do tend to bite off more than you can chew, and chew it anyway. But that's not a bad thing!" Joe said one afternoon as we sat on opposite ends of our bed, deep in conversation about my upcoming travel plans—which we agreed would mean the end of our relationship.

I looked down and scratched the scruff between Kitty's shoulder blades as she lied curled up between us. She sleepily lifted a single eyelid, accompanied by a tiny, irritated "meow," before tucking her soft tootsies and then flopping heavily onto her other side. She twisted her chin up toward the ceiling, paws hanging loosely against her upper belly like an upright bunny. I kept my eyes cast down at the impression Kitty's petite tabby body left on the comforter, and said, "So, you're sure you don't want to come with me?"

Two and a half years had passed since our first date at Bukowski Tavern on Dalton Street. "I'm sorry, but no. I'm definitely not interested in traveling for that long. And you know I don't care that much about vegan food," said Joe.

It's not like I was asking a lot of him—just to, you know, uproot his life, leave a new job he loved, and live out of a vehicle for an indefinite period of time, in the name of an adventure that only I was passionate about.

"Yeah," I said softly, lifting my view—one set of teary eyes meeting another.

Joe sort of became vegan, for about a week, one time while we were together. It was actually at another event featuring George Eisman, the dietitian who woke me up to veganism years earlier. Joe said he was shaken by the dairy facts he'd learned that day. However, without strong convictions to continue, he understandably had little interest in the road trip.

While it would be a lot easier to blame the gradual decline of our relationship on his non-vegan-ness, or on my desire to travel full-time, the truth is that we had already experienced a few rough patches in the years prior, some that I thought for sure would end things on their own. But, out of what I now believe to have been comfort and convenience, we carried on.

Despite all this—and my looming historical relationship-ending timeline—I still wanted Joe by my side during the trip. I still asked him, many times, to please consider joining me. But I see now that it wasn't coming from a place of deep love or commitment to Joe, but a place of fear. Fear of change, of the unknown, and of being alone physically and emotionally.

I clutched the gear shift that jutted out to the right side just behind the steering wheel, pulled it slightly toward me, and then moved it four clicks to the left, settling the orange oblong indicator on top of the letter P. Gerty hummed and I rotated the engine key toward me until she quietly settled.

Philly.

It was a fairly warm, late afternoon in mid-March and it was my first time visiting Philly for more than an hour. The sun playfully bounced off of and rolled between the clouds, making its way through Gerty's windshield as I peered out, scoping the surrounding neighborhood for an initial 'potential overnight' safety assessment.

· Ja-ja-ja-ja-jig. With The Club locked into place, I raised the right side green-clothed armrest, swiveled, and crouched as I scooted between and then behind the driver and passenger seats. I drew the dividing blackout curtains and flopped belly-first onto the bed.

"Vegan coffee wifi," I tapped into the Yelp! app's search bar. "Grindcore House," appeared at the top. "Coffee and tea, vegan, vegetarian," read the sub categories. Elated to see the word "vegan" appear effortlessly, I clicked through to learn that Grindcore House didn't offer just a few vegan options, but was in fact a 100% vegan establishment. I couldn't help but audibly "Eeeeeeee." I scrambled to close up Gerty and go check out this dream of a coffee shop.

"Ah, here we are, 4th and Greenwich." It was just a few blocks from where I had parked the van. I looked up from the digital map on my phone to see a brightly painted red brick exterior accented by black wooden window frames, and a tall, narrow set of double doors facing the intersection.

I was greeted by a shiny, beckoning display case filled with cannolis, cupcakes, scones, cookies, muffins, pies, donuts, cakes, whoopie pies, and bottled drinks. To the right, a coffee station offering soy, almond, coconut, and rice milk and creamers.

Heaven.

I was excited and ready to go all-in, so I ordered an almond milk mocha latte topped with soy whipped cream, drizzled with chocolate syrup, and dusted with cocoa powder and cinnamon. Oh, and a cannoli for good measure.

As someone who doesn't particularly like coffee, I was well on my way to developing a taste for it.

I explored a short hallway that led to the back room—a bright, naturally lit space filled with dozens of tables and chairs and a large couch, the walls covered in local art, and of course grindcore music pumping through the shop's sound system.

"Mocha latte for Kristin," the petite blonde, tattooed barista shouted from the front counter.

"Thank you so much! Hey, do you guys have free Wi-Fi here?" I asked.

"We sure do!"

Score.

Grindcore House would not only become my preferred hotspot for caffeine and sugar fixes, but it would also become my temporary Philly-based office, and where I'd start every morning, to piddle and to brush my teeth.

This would be my life for the next 18 months: washing up in public restrooms, selecting virtual offices by way of their Wi-Fi access and nondairy creamer options, and sometimes even getting a shower in when possible (more on that later).

It was far from any way of life I'd known or expected to ever embody.

I lifted the wide cup's edge to my lips, closed my eyes, and sipped with slow deliberateness. Slurp.

I had never before been more okay—and more ready—to be alone.

CHAPTER 7

CONTRAST

I woke up early the following morning, excited to finally take time from focused eating to explore a bit of the city's touristy sights. After catching up on email while enjoying a Grindcore House bagel—slathered with their homemade black olive and herb cream cheese—I strolled along bustling South Street, visited the sparkly Magic Gardens, awed at the eclecticism of Atomic City Comics, and perused the narrow aisles of Repo Records. I made my way to the petite, historically beautiful Elfreth's Alley, and waited in line to snap a photo of the Liberty Bell.

While leisurely strolling down Walnut Street, soaking up the squint-inducing St. Patrick's Day sun, on my way to an early dinner, I passed a homeless woman holding a sign that read, "I'm pregnant, hungry, and alone."

I felt a rush of heat and pain come over my body that made me want to drop to my knees in front of her, and dig through my backpack in search of every penny I could find. But, as I had conditioned myself to do, my mind instead began questioning the truth of the lettering on the piece of cardboard propped in front of her. 'She doesn't look pregnant,' I thought to myself. 'How did she become homeless to begin with? Maybe she's addicted to drugs or alcohol. If she is pregnant, how will the baby survive?' These thoughts quickly pushed out the urgency I had originally felt to help her.

I kept walking.

When I turned to face the direction of my momentum, I was immediately stopped by a young man with a huge grin.

"Hi. My name is Todd. Do you care about the environment?" he queried. Had I not been distracted by the maybe-pregnant homeless woman, I would have sooner spotted the mission worker and preemptively crossed the street to avoid the awkward side-glance smile thing that I would have given, followed by a lowered head nod and a "Sorry, I've got to get to where I'm going," type of response that I'd forced upon dozens of other solicitors from streets past.

Before I knew it, he was sharing details about rain forests and environmental conservation.

"I do care!" I blurted out, to my surprise. 'Oh here we go. Now what have I started? This is going to take forever,' I thought to myself.

"That's wonderful!" said Todd.

"Um. Yeah, I've been vegan for more than five years now." I said. "And since I'm not supporting the meat and dairy industries—which I believe are responsible for so much environmental destruction on the planet, what with the methane gases produced by livestock farts, the millions of acres of land destroyed to house and feed the animals that we kill for food—their food that could of course go to feed starving people around the world instead of the animals—I feel like, by eating a plant-based diet, I'm contributing to the preventative measures necessary to help save the planet," I said.

I think we were both surprised as we stood in silence for a minute before Todd said, "Oh. Well that's cool! Are you interested in donating anyway?" Todd seemed like a nice enough kid, so I filled out the form and handed him some cash.

"Sweet. Thanks, Kristin. Here's your receipt," he said. Todd continued, "So, are you not from around here?"

I went on to tell Todd about the road trip, how I was driving, writing, and eating my way through the country, by way of vegan restaurants, cafés, and food trucks.

"Dude, that's really cool. Good on ya!" he said. "Well, it was great to meet you, Kristin. Good luck on your travels!" And with a graceful about-face, Todd had just as quickly stopped his next potential donor.

I somehow felt lighter after my conversation with Todd. I don't know if it was because I finally stopped and talked with one of these activists who, up until that point, only ever made me an anxious street jumper. Maybe it was because I finally voiced my opinion on a cause that does really matter to me, and to someone who maybe had a shared interest. I'm not sure. It did, for some reason or another, cause me to turn around.

Before swinging my pack over my shoulder, and slipping my left arm through the strap, I dug into the tiny inner pocket flap and pulled out a five-dollar bill, walked back to the pregnant woman, knelt down, and dropped it into the clear plastic to-go container next to her.

"Thank you, thank you, thank you so much, ma'am," she said. For the first time, I made and held eye contact with the pregnant homeless woman. I felt the warmth and anguish come back.

"You're welcome," I said.

A left on South 12th and a right on Locust Street, and there it was: Vedge Restaurant.

The hype around this relatively new, completely vegan establishment was pretty grand, so naturally my expectations were low, since I had learned early on that buzz didn't always equate to quality, but just more so fed the chatter.

Before walking up the steps and into the first doorway, I stopped and looked down at myself. I was wearing a pair of navy Toms shoes, green capri khakis, a black t-shirt that said, "flesh is for zombies," with a picture of a cute, little exposed-brain zombie head, and a black-and-red schoolyard backpack, busting at its seams.

Classy.

I lifted an arm and took a whiff. Nope. Not good. It had been five days since my last shower, and after this sweaty, tourist-filled day, it was beginning to show.

Thanks to Chris M., one of the restaurant's pastry chefs with whom I had enjoyed chatting over lattes a few days prior, I had a reservation. As it turns out, one needs a reservation for a restaurant of this caliber, but unfortunately that meant I had to walk in as-is. No time to find a place to shower or to freshen up.

I walked up to the hostess stand and was greeted by two women wearing crisp, matching uniforms. Another woman approached, wearing a beautiful fitted pantsuit. I shrank a little, grabbing the left shoulder strap of the pack with my right hand in an effort to casually cover up the wordplay on my shirt.

"Welcome to Vedge, Kristin. Let me show you to your table." I was momentarily in awe that the woman knew my first name, before realizing that my reservation—as made by one of their staff—was likely the reason.

She escorted me past the first room containing a gorgeous, wood paneled bar that stretched the length of the entire room. Its glossy, granite surface reflected the light from the dozens of bulbs fixated within black triangular wire caging from above, the far walls lined with neat rows of bottles of wine.

We walked into the next room, and turned right. The pantsuit-ed woman gestured toward a tall table for two.

"Will this do?" she asked.

"Oh yes, this is great. Thanks!" I said.

I squeezed my shoulder blades together and shimmied the pack off, set it under the table next to the dark wood paneled molding that lined the floor, and lifted myself into the tall chair.

With a slow exhale, I quietly settled in, snug against the wall, hoping no one would notice my stinky pits as they passed by. The narrow, dimly lit room—home to stunning deep auburn wood fixtures and accents, and dotted with cozy seating throughout—kept my eyes dancing from one end to the other. In front of me, the far room opened to a larger, almost living room-like space with bigger tables, a crackling fireplace, and tall, stained glass windows. To my right lay an exposed kitchen prep area with gleaming countertops and matching bowls, plates, and select cutlery.

"Welcome to Vedge. Here are our menus. Please let me know if you have any questions," the smartly dressed server said.

"Thank you so much," I replied.

I started with the pomegranate sangria, a blend of pomegranate juice and liquor with cubed pieces of apples and oranges, and a single cinnamon stick. For the next hour, I indulged in Vedge's tantalizingly smoky sweet potato pate; a sampler platter—brought out and presented by the head chef and co-owner himself—featuring paper-thin sliced mushrooms with red onion and capers, a playful line of avocado, tofu, rosemary sauce, finely diced white onions, and chopped root vegetables; and a pair of the most deliciously seasoned, sweet, melt-in-your-mouth carrots accompanied by a white bean dip that hinted of a pickled zest.

Next, a small triangular plate piled with the most stunning shaved brussels sprouts—their tangy tenderness warranting a single raised brow followed by feverish fork pointing and head nodding—dominated my palate and camera phone.

And set in a light orange sauce, hugged by a bed of lentils and spiced green onions, was Vedge's succulent house-made seitan.

"This powerful combination of veggies left an impression like no other. I'm in love and lost for words. I want more yet somehow feel satisfied at the same time. I'm mesmerized by the quality of taste, the consistency of every dish, and the care that has clearly gone into prepping and plating the meals. Stunning.

Delicious. Innovative. Perfect," I wrote on my phone's Notes app—in preparation for the forthcoming blog post that would feature this meal and my time spent in Philly.

"I'll take these plates out of your way," the attentive server said as she swooped by, holding one armful of plates already. She leaned in and asked, "Would you like anything for dessert?"

With a tight-lipped grin, I asked, "Hmmm, what would you recommend?"

"Right now, my personal favorite is the lemon cheesecake round complemented by a blood orange sauce," she said.

"Sold!" I replied.

My fork slid prongs-first through the side of the cheesecake like a warm knife in nondairy butter, pausing momentarily to request more pressure to cut through the graham cracker crust that lined the base. If it were possible to fall in love with food, this would be my moment. My eyes flirted with the creamy dollop of cake that lingered seductively along the curved edges of the fork. Like a trained commercial actress, I raised the sweet cake to my lips, moved the fork slowly into my mouth, then pressed my lips together. I took a deep breath in, closed my eyes, and let out an "mmmmm," as I carefully withdrew the fork. The lemon cheesecake swirled, tempted the roof of my mouth and inside of my cheeks, and titillated every taste bud on my tongue.

When I regained consciousness, I had nearly polished off the entire piece of cheesecake. I re-opened the Notes app and added a few words: "Wow, wow, wow!"

Drunk with a food coma, I staggered out to the Philadelphia streets, now swarming with green-clad, tipsy St. Patrick's Day revelers.

The two-mile walk back to the van felt longer that night as the sun began to set. In the final handful of blocks, the streetlights turned on in unison with a buzz, and my eyelids involuntarily blinked every few feet as I passed beneath the yellowy-orange triangular streams of florescent light that soaked the sidewalk.

I rounded the corner at South 5th and Gerrit Street, where Gerty waited patiently. Before approaching the van, I looked down the street to the left, and then to the right. And I glanced behind me to be sure no one was watching. After unlocking the set of side doors, I pressed the square black button in and pulled the larger of the two conjoined doors open, toward me.

The narrow plastic step at the van's base squeaked under the pressure as I used it to step up, heaving my upper body and backpack into the van. I quickly pulled the door shut and immediately pushed the lock horizontally into place, the orange strip within the door panel disappearing to indicate "locked."

I slid the backpack off my right shoulder, then the other, gently onto the floor. My life was in that pack. Everything that kept me in touch with the world. My phone, my computer, and the keys to this van. I sat heavily onto the edge of the bed, and then fell back onto the mattress.

I swung my arms up above my head and reached for the built-in wooden coat rack. I liked to think I could do pull-ups on it, but never tried for fear it would crack over my face. Sometimes it served as a nice upper body stretcher.

Oof. I smell.

I picked up my phone and selected the 'settings' option, then 'wallpaper and brightness,' and moved the indicator node to the left to dim the screen. I opened my email and scanned the new messages.

"RE: shower in Philly," the notification from my Couch Surfing account read. A reply had come in from Kim, a friendly couch surfer who had offered up her bathroom for an hour so that I could take a shower.

Thank goodness.

One at a time—heel to toe—I kicked off my Toms, set my phone on silent, and rolled, heavy as a sack of sand, onto my left side, pulling my favorite heavy brown comforter atop of me. Too tired to change out of my stinky clothes, I tucked my legs and body into a fetal curl, and fell asleep to the comfort of a full belly, a warm heart, and the promise of a shower the next day.

CHAPTER 8

IL WAITER

"When you're a loner, there's nothing more
satisfying than finding another loner, to be alone with."

THE AMERICANS

"The manager tells me you're on quite the adventure," he said, setting down a plate of romaine-wrapped raw tacos and a mason jar of sangria.

I looked up from the menu to see a valiant twenty-something man dressed in all black. He stood up straight and clasped his hands behind him, his wavy, dark brown hair slicked neatly back, except for a single curl that sat provocatively to the left of his brow. There was a dark, alluring way about him that caused me to look away almost as soon as I'd first met his gaze.

"Oh. My name is Luca. I'll be your server tonight," he said, with a slight bow forward.

"Hi. Oh. Yes, I'm Kristin. Um. Yeah, I've been traveling for a few months. Living out of a van. Just landed in the area yesterday," I said.

"Nice," he replied. "So, the owner of the restaurant isn't here tonight, but she told me to bring out a few samples of a bunch of our stuff. So, I'll stop by in a few after you've had a chance to try the tacos."

"Cool. Sounds good. Thanks," I said. He lingered for a minute, adding a slight smirk, before turning to walk away.

I blushed immediately and glanced at the family of four sitting at the table next to me, wondering if they too had caught that brief glimpse of chemistry—or if I had only imagined it.

It had been a few days since my last shower. My hair was pulled back into a high, greasy ponytail, I had no makeup on, and knew I was beginning to stink. Despite this, under the unexpected attention of the waiter, I suddenly felt sexier than ever. I sat up a little taller and pulled a book out of my pack so that I could appear busy and studious, even though I was really blushing below the surface and thinking about what I'd say when Luca returned with the next course.

He came back a few minutes later with a plate of nachos and a portobello mushroom dish. "Here we go," he said.

"Wow, I'm definitely not going to be able to eat all of this," I said.

"Yeah. Well the good news is you can always take the leftovers to-go," Luca replied. We exchanged smiles—mine shyer than his—and again he lingered for a minute, and then said, "I just got back from a bit of traveling too."

"Yeah?" I queried.

"Yeah. I spent three months cycling across Italy. Visited some family there. It was awesome."

"Wow. That sounds amazing," I said.

"Maybe we can share our travel stories sometime," he added. I smiled a little bigger, managing this time to hold Luca's penetrating gaze.

"That would be great," I said.

Luca returned again, this time with a hot fudge, pomegranate seed, chopped walnut, and soy whip-covered sundae.

"Oh my goodness!" I said, as my eyes widened. I didn't want him to know I was way too full for dessert, but planned to down the entire thing anyway.

"Enjoy!" he said. As I looked up to catch Luca's stare, his eyes darted away, and then back again. With his view momentarily at the floor, he took a step closer, leaned on the table with one hand, gestured with the other, and said, "A few of us usually go out for drinks after work. You're welcome to join."

I wrote my number down and handed it to him, and then he looked at me in a Bill Compton to Sookie Stackhouse kind of way. I thought he might take me right there, in the middle of the restaurant. I interrupted the thought with a, "It was great to meet you. Keep me in the loop for later."

"Will do," said Luca.

I coolly walked out of the restaurant into the crisp night air, turned the corner and, once out of sight of the restaurant windows, bolted to the van, jumped in, and zoomed off to the hotel I'd booked earlier that day.

Controlled panic set in as I threw fresh clothes into my pack, trotted into the hotel, pressed the elevator button a dozen times, and then jogged to my room. 'It's okay. It's okay. I probably won't even hear from him. It was just some innocent flirting,' I thought.

I stripped down and had one foot in the shower when I heard my phone vibrate against the ceramic tile of the bathroom sink. A text message had come in from a number I didn't recognize. When I opened it, it read: "Hey Kristin! It's Luca, from the restaurant. I'm just getting out of work now. You still interested in meeting up for a bit?"

Even though I was all a fluster while showering, and getting ready to go hang out with a complete stranger—one whom I was sure was interested in more than just hanging out—I didn't really know what to expect. I'd never in my life been picked up by a stranger, let alone a server at a restaurant. Or, had I picked him up?

I made myself wait to reply to Luca's text message until I finished showering. I didn't want to seem too eager, of course. Then I replied, "Of course! :) This is my first time in the area so I'll leave it up to you as to where we should go."

My heartbeat skipped as I drew nearer to the market where Luca was having a post-work meal. I entered and passed the clerk, then headed up the stairway to the seating area. As I crested the stairs, I saw Luca sitting alone, eating from a to-go box.

He somehow looked even more dashing now, in a grey newsboy cap and plaid button-down.

"Hey," I said nonchalantly, as I approached. But I couldn't hide my nervous smile.

"Hey, Kristin! Good to see you," he said, before taking another bite of some kind of mixed greens salad.

"Oh, your friends didn't make it?" I asked.

"Oh, no one else felt like going out tonight. I hope you don't mind if it's just the two of us," he said.

"Not at all."

I was secretly elated that it'd be just us. There's not a single part of me that felt nervous, in a bad or fearful way. From the moment his energy bubble touched mine at the restaurant, I felt comfortable—and mysteriously unhinged, in the most amazing way—around this stunning Italian man.

Our shared energy was palpable yet subtle as we ambled to a wine bar a few blocks away. I couldn't help but notice Luca's incredibly calm and collected demeanor. It didn't seem cocky or off-putting, but more comfortable, and casual. It was nice, and made it easy to settle into conversation.

Even though it was a weekend night, the dimly lit, charming garden-level bar wasn't at all crowded. We sat facing each other at a quaint table for two. It was perfect.

With wineglass after wineglass in hand, I swooned over Luca's fanciful stories about his incredible bicycle tour through Italy, the people he'd met, his love of travel, and closeness to his family. He talked of his pre-waiter ventures as a professional mariner on tall ships for wealthy, private yacht owners. He spoke about being vegetarian, and the kicker: how much he enjoyed dancing. But it was when Luca shared one of his favorite stories—of how his grandparents met and fell in love, over dance—that it was all I could do to keep from reaching across the table and pulling his lips to mine. I wanted to feel him against me, his arms around my waist, and to breathe him in. He needn't say any more. I was beyond enchanted. And I think he knew it.

I don't remember the series of events that led us to my hotel room that night, other than knowing I had to pee badly during our walk back, and that there was likely nowhere to stop and go, now that it was 2AM.

"That's Chuck…" Luca said, as we passed by a maroon Volvo wagon "…my car. And don't let the name fool you; she's a she," he said with a laugh.

"Oooh, well, she's beautiful," I said.

'Between the dancing, the traveling, and the car-naming, could we be any more alike?' I thought. Well, I knew we could. What did I really know about him after only a few hours of tipsy-laden dreamy talk anyway? But, in this moment, he'd hit all of my trigger points, and that was enough.

Why we didn't stop at Chuck to contemplate Luca's departure, I do not know. Soon we were quietly tucked into separate corners of the elevator, throwing bashful glances at each other while waiting for the doors to open at the fifth floor.

With Luca close behind, I briskly walked down the hallway, unlocked the door with the plastic key card, and hurried into the bathroom.

"GOT ANY GOOD SALSA MUSIC WE COULD DANCE TO?" Luca shouted, from the main room.

"UM. NOT SURE. BE RIGHT OUT," I shouted back.

I stared at myself in the mirror while washing my hands. I'd never even come close to having a one-night stand before.

I didn't know if that's what this would be, if anything at all. But we were here. In a hotel. I was eager. And a bit nervous.

———————

In general, I'd always carried a negative association with casual intimacy. Few of my friends have ever opened up to me about their non-monogamous *sexcapades*, and it's no wonder— I'm pretty certain my responses were of a judgmental tone: 'How could you? Why would you? What about love? What about STDs?' etc.

It was when I was apartment hunting in Boston about four years earlier that I first began to really question the constructs of traditional relationships. I'd met Aaron, who had a room for rent in his home. Despite a lack of outward flirting during the house tour, there was immediate and undeniable chemistry between us. Before I returned home that night, I had gotten an email from him inviting me out to a bar with him and his friends.

I took it upon myself to do some Facebook stalking before replying, and that's when I saw his status: "In an open relationship with Jennifer." I'd never considered the term, or the idea of it, before. An *open relationship*. It seems silly and closed-minded now, looking back. But it was my truth at the time.

I told Aaron I'd discovered he was in a relationship, which opened a world of new dialogue between us. Both he and Jennifer were very forthcoming about their relationship—how and why it worked, what didn't, and all they'd learned together. I was intrigued. His pursuit of me culminated in an outing with just Jennifer, so she could assess her comfort level, and if she'd be cool with me dating and/or sleeping with Aaron. It turned out I wasn't quite ready for that dynamic. I never did anything with Aaron other than chat over lunch at a restaurant once, but it certainly served to wake me up, and shake me out of the mindset I'd been carrying all my life: that casual sex is wrong, and that monogamy is the only way.

Shortly after that experience, I met Joe, and so for the time being that explorative chapter—and related exploration—had closed. But now I was open to experiencing something new, and the sexy Italian server was waiting for me in the other room.

I gave my hair one last jush, and picked out my makeup-covered eye crusts, before leaving the bathroom. Luca was standing in the middle of the room, his hands in his pockets. With a slight head tilt, he looked up at me from under the brim of his cap, and in a single, nearly involuntary motion, I confidently strode over, put my hands through his thick hair, and pulled his lips to mine.

I felt his arms wrap around my waist, and a hand move up the center of my back, our bodies now against one another.

He kissed me sweetly as I ran a hand firmly along the base of his neckline, pulling him in for a deeper kiss this time. My attention moved from our lips to notice and feel his hands now resting on my hips, his fingers lightly dancing below my shirt, just above my pant line.

I never did put music on, but as we continued to kiss standing in the middle of the hotel room—familiarizing ourselves with each other's rhythms, sensitivities, and cadences—we began to sway. Slowly. And just a little. When I realized we'd begun moving to whatever silent tempo we shared, I tucked my chin and snickered.

"What?" Luca whispered, with a smile, now moving his hands down over my backside.

"I just noticed we're swaying to no music at all," I said quietly.

"Yeah. It's nice, isn't it?" he asked.

"Mmmhmm," I replied, our noses touching playfully as we talked so closely.

We kissed, caressed, grabbed, and petted like this for a while until Luca turned us together, and backed me up to the foot of the bed. In what seemed like the slowest form possible, he guided me down to my back, and then kissed his way up my body until we were nose-to-nose again. As the energy livened, so too did the exploration of our hands—now reaching for more daring distances.

I began unbuttoning Luca's shirt, and he my pants, between kisses. He moved down my body and stood at the end of the bed, sliding both hands down one of my legs.

"Man, you double knot your shoes?" he said with a laugh, trying to untie them.

"Naturally," I said. "They *always* come untied if I don't!" We laughed together as Luca continued to struggle with the knots in my shoelaces before finally flinging them off.

The remaining layers of our clothing came off more quickly now. We helped each other, and we helped ourselves, until there was nothing but bed sheets between us.

"So, tell me more about Italy," I said, weaving an index finger through Luca's light chest hair.

We hadn't fallen asleep until well after four in the morning. As we woke slowly now, to curling in and around one another, to morning stretches and yawns, we chatted with raspy voices about our respective past and future travels.

"I'm going to be in Puerto Rico the week after next, for a wedding. If you're feeling adventurous, you should meet me there. It'd be a short two-day trip, but would be super romantic and fun!" he said.

The late morning sun peeked through a break in the curtains as Luca began massaging my head. I nearly fell back asleep until he kissed my forehead, and then my neck. I rolled over and shaped my body to his, pulled his arms around me, and placed his hands on my chest. It didn't take long before we were all over one another again, falling into a quick romp.

Luca left before noon for a CPR training course. He'd been working on an AmeriCorps application and needed to be certified for it. We said our goodbyes and I checked out of the hotel, then headed to a coffee shop to answer emails and work on the next blog post. I'd forgotten to leave Will Travel... stickers at the restaurant the night before—I'd been a bit distracted—so I asked Luca if he'd be able to meet up later, to retrieve them.

"So, do I get to see this awesome van of yours?" Luca asked, over a cup of coffee..

"Yeah, of course," I replied.

I added a few quarters to Gerty's meter and then invited Luca inside for the grand tour.

"Sooo, yeah. That's pretty much it. This is where I live." I said. Luca was sitting on the wooden chest and I on the edge of the van's bed. I expected him to say something in return, but instead he stood hunched over, stepped forward, and started kissing me gently.

I pulled him down onto me, rolled us over, and then sat up—as much as I could, given the limited girth of Gerty. Luca reached up under my plaid dress and slipped my tights down from the waist as I pulled his shirt up and off.

We spent the next hour rolling and thrusting around the van. When we'd hear someone walk by, we'd freeze and cover each other's mouths, giggling quietly.

Throughout that hour, I'd have moments of clarity where I was so thankful for having been open to meeting Luca, and to these jaunts with him. It was fun and sweet and sexy as hell. It was one of the most impromptu and exciting sexual experiences I'd ever had.

There's something incredibly invigorating about yielding to a new way of viewing, and acting on, an aspect of one's life— particularly one that had once felt firmly set in stone for so long.

I was beginning to understand that this experience with Luca was less about the supposed randomness of it all, and more about giving myself permission to try something new—something outside my comfort zone—without cruel self-judgment, bias, or resentment. It was far more meaningful than it initially appeared. And for that, I am so grateful. ·

I had to get on the road before nightfall, but I really wanted to stay. Even though Luca was kind and giving, in the 18 or so hours that we'd known each other, what made it easier to say goodbye was this unspoken emotional unavailability that seemed to lie just below his surface.

I struggled with it at first, unable to understand where it was coming from—and not yet comfortable enough to ask. But I also liked the idea of keeping our interaction relatively light. Maybe that's what it was for him too. And maybe that's why he seemed a bit distant, despite our jolly romps.

Everything about the few hours that passed—from the time I sat in his section of the restaurant to the moment we said goodbye a second time—had been so hugely different from anything I'd ever experienced. I didn't want to ruin it with over-analyzing. I wanted to leave things just as they were: an incredibly steamy, sort-of one-night stand, with an adventurous, slightly younger, sexy, somewhat emotionally unavailable Italian waiter.

CHAPTER 9

GUARDED

'Bang, bang, bang.'
'Bang, bang, bang, BANG!'

The bursts of noise crept into my dream, rocking me awake. As my brain attempted to make sense of the rattles, I realized I wasn't dreaming — as I had, so many times before, had nightmares about Gerty being broken into, waking to a dark figure standing over me. My voice would inevitably falter. I'd try to scream, but nothing would come out. I'd keep trying to yell and flail and throw fists, until I'd panic myself awake. Despite keeping a can of mace on one side of my pillow, and a hammer on the other, just in case it'd come to that, I'd have this same dream two to three nights a week, for almost the full 18 months I lived in the van.

But this was real; one of my biggest road trip fears had come true, short of someone actually making their way into the van. My brain registered positive as my eyes shot open to the fact that indeed someone was very loudly knocking on the van's side doors.

New Jersey, Maryland, and Delaware were behind me and I was now in Washington, D.C., wrapping up the foodie rounds indulging in the country's best faux fried chicken sandwiches from Everlasting Life, deliciously unique soups from SouperGirl, fantastic diner-style eats from Busboys & Poets, and coma-inducing pastries from Sticky Fingers Bakery.

I managed to squeeze in D.C.'s eight or so vegan eateries within a few frantic days, since this district had already presented a series of irritants. Within the first day of my D.C. stopover, I lost my driver's license, received a very expensive parking ticket, and then the van's starter died, causing me to miss a dinner meet-up, and one restaurant entirely since they were a reservation-only establishment.

All this after being threatened with arrest by a café owner in New Jersey a few days earlier. I'd spent the entire day working from this great vegan food and juice bar in New Brunswick. They had Wi-Fi, and it was a laid-back atmosphere. I'd asked if I could hang out and work.

Feeling a bit under the weather that day, I departed the café, found a quiet side street, and retired for a few in the back of the van. The moment my head hit the pillow, my stomach dropped as I realized I'd forgotten to pay my bill. No one was attending the café when I'd walked out; paying somehow slipped my mind! I called the café right away, and the conversation went something like this:

Me: Hi, this is Kristin from the vegan travel blog. I just left there and…

Café owner: Oh, did you get pulled over?

Me: Um. No. I was just calling to say…

Café owner: Did the cops find you? You didn't pay and I called the cops.

Me: Oh my gosh. No. That's why I'm calling. I'm so sorry. I completely forgot to pay and I'm headed back there right now.

Café owner: Well I hope so. The cops are here waiting for you.

Me: I'm so sorry! This has never happened before. I'll be right over.

There *was* a cop at the café when I returned. Though she was a regular, and the owner hadn't actually called anyone. He tried turning it into a joke after we settled the bill. Still, it left me feeling terrible and a bit shaken.

"So, you drive around the country, by yourself, just to eat food?" asked John, the tow truck driver, as we pulled away, Gerty's wheels chained to the bed of his tow truck. She looked uncharacteristically small compared to the Transformer she now rode upon. It was Easter Sunday and I was convinced that no one would be available to assist me, that I'd be stranded on the corner of Rittenhouse and 3rd Street Northwest for the night. At least I'd have the leftovers from Senbeb Café to keep me from going hungry. But I called AAA and, to my delight, they sent John right over.

"Yeah. I've been at it for a few months now. It's pretty great," I said to John.

"That's very cool, young lady. That takes mighty courage, you know," he said.

We continued to chat about my travels, his family plans for later that day, vegan food spotting, and decided together what my best options were for getting the van looked at during the holiday.

I sat on the far passenger side of the cab's stiff, springy bucket seat—feeling a bit out of place in my black-and-white polka dot summer dress and flip flops—hugged by a grey seatbelt that had been darkened around the buckle and shoulder area, presumably by hardworking hands, and proceeded to make a series of phone calls to find a mechanic that would be able to take a look at the van the same day.

We pulled into the nearest open NTB, which ended up being just across the border, in Maryland. Admittedly, I felt intimidated and put off by the way the male employees were looking in my direction and whispering to one another. For a moment, I wondered if I'd left any unmentionables out in the open, on the floor of the van or something. Or if they were simply trying to piece together what this short little lady and her odd, bed-in-the-back New York State-plated van with vegan and animal rights stickers all over the place were doing.

Noticing my discomfort, John approached the five men who stood huddled together inspecting the van. I don't know what he said to them, but he walked over to me after and gave me his cell number; "In case these guys give you any grief," he said. "They should take good care of you though. I told them what I think is wrong with the van and they should have it fixed and ready for you later today."

"Thank you so much!" I said as John climbed back into the tow truck. Part of me wished he'd stay until everything was sorted. But, with a final head nod, a series of intermittent beeps accompanied the truck as it backed out of the lot and drove away. I looked down at the new number in my phone, and squeezed it tightly.

As it happened, it was too late in the day for NTB to obtain the parts needed to repair Gerty. So I collected my backpack, computer, and some clothes, shoved some of the electronics into their secret compartment under the bed, grabbed the container of leftovers, and found a hotel to hole up in for the night within walking distance. Thanks to Priceline's "Name Your Own Price" deal, I was able to stay at a fairly fancy hotel for less than $50. Score!

Staying at hotels—which I would do every so often if I needed a long overdue shower or simply a rare reprieve from van-dwelling—meant the most amazing, scalding hot evening showers and pillow nests. Nothing beats sinking into a good U-shaped pillow fort to feel comforted, safe, and warm—especially when spending so much time on my own.

The next morning, I received a call from Dave at NTB; the van would be ready by noon. I went to the bathroom, washed my face, and brushed my teeth—*ahhh*, a real bathroom—and then propped a couple pillows against the headboard of the queen size bed. I pulled the blankets up around my waist and situated a pillow on my lap as a mock tabletop. I opened my computer, and began mapping out my trek through West Virginia and Virginia.

Step one: open the vegan restaurant spreadsheet that Eric from the Happy Cow resource guide sent my way at the beginning of the trip. Scroll to state in question and systematically Google every restaurant on the list to check first to see if they're still open, then check the hours of operation and location; add to Google maps. Step two: search Google for, "vegan in West Virginia;" compare notes from Happy Cow spreadsheet. Step three: search, "vegan + West Virginia," within Yelp.com; compare notes from Happy Cow spreadsheet and Google search. Step four: search the VegDining.com website; cross-reference with previous notes. And step five: share preliminary list on the Will Travel for Vegan Food Facebook page to ask my friends if I had overlooked any vegan eateries. Depending on the state, or even a given city, this process could take up to eight or more hours at a time.

Since West Virginia and Virginia had only a combined dozen or so vegan restaurants between them—zero being in West Virginia and twelve or so in Virginia—it took just two or three hours to walk through the five-step process and determine locations before mapping out a route that would enable me to continue heading south.

———

'BANG! BANG!'

The knocks came louder and more impatiently this time. Now fully alert and partially afraid to move, I quietly searched the blankets for my glasses and then slunk to the floor and moved toward the closed divider curtains. I carefully poked a finger through the curtains to catch a reflection off the passenger side view mirror.

The night before, I had parked closer to the city, next to a crowded metered spot that was set to start charging again at six in the morning. So, I set an alarm for 5:50AM and drearily drove to this specific parking lot because there was a Starbucks I intended to work out of most of the day—writing for the blog, replying to email inquiries, and mapping out the next portion of the trip.

By the time I pulled into the empty lot—shared by a large grocery store on one end, a restaurant, and a few smaller shops, including the Starbucks, on the other—I was in no way ready to start the day. I hadn't even changed out of my PJs for the short drive from the city meter to the outskirts parking lot. Like I had done just a few times prior, I parked the van in the lot, closed her up, dove headfirst onto the bed, and curled into the blankets to catch a few more Z's before officially rising for the day ahead.

Shortly after leaving D.C., I'd learn that the folks at the Maryland NTB had simply cleaned and then re-installed the starter I came in with, despite charging me for a new one. The van would miraculously carry me through West Virginia—where the lack of vegan eateries led me to instead hike a teensy portion of the Appalachian Trail and spend a night in one of the seediest hotels I've ever been to—and on through Virginia, before it would die out again, leaving the next mechanic to gently break the news about how I'd been duped.

It had also been three months and seven and a half states since Nate and I went our separate ways. Since then, we had been in touch every so often. We emailed and texted on occasion, even chatted over the phone a few times, about working through our differences, and reconnecting over our shared love of sci-fi/action adventure movies. It was nice, and felt like we were making real steps toward mending our sensitive friendship. But, every now and then, we'd have another blowout argument. Sometimes it was a simple miscommunication, quickly resolved. Other times it was waking up to dozens of texts or emails with violent accusations: that I'm only able to do this because I have lady parts and therefore people are more willing to be kind, that he was let go of the trip unceremoniously, that I was sleeping with every male I encountered, that I had been selfish and used him to get where I was, or that I hadn't given him enough credit for all he'd done.

It was a constant up-and-down. Happy and sad. Light and dark. Much like when we were traveling together. I know I contributed as well—I'm not claiming innocence here. I wasn't always yielding or open. I am in no way a victim in the matter. In fact, I'm beginning to realize that I had created this experience for myself out of necessity, and that perhaps all of this was very important, not only to push me to do the road trip alone, but also to highlight areas that needed attention—the kind of attention and care that could only come from within.

Plus, I'd like to believe that every person I've encountered serves a greater purpose than just kind of being there. That there's a bigger reason we were brought together. No matter how seemingly insignificant the interaction, or how much time is spent together, I can look back at all of my romantic relationships, loves, friendships, and acquaintances and find something in those pairings that changed me in some way. In some cases it took years to see, but, at the end of it—when I'd have time to reflect and give myself permission to be open to the lessons—I could see exactly why said person came into my life.

But for now, with Nate, it was simply too much; I knew we couldn't continue on this way. It wasn't healthy, and it seemed as though we were holding each other down instead of healing or helping each other at all. So, late one night, after yet another series of anger-filled, hurtful emails, I decided it would be best if we parted on all levels this time.

I messaged Nate and explained that it was simply too difficult—this back-and-forth—and that I was going to stop following him on social media so that we could formally let go of each other. Unfortunately this set off one of his harshest reactions yet. It was after midnight when my phone began buzzing second after second with an abrupt word or three about what a terrible person I was.

In that moment, I felt like I was back in Chicago, utterly helpless and afraid to make a peep. I panicked and blocked Nate's number, and blocked him on social media too. And then, through my foggy, tear-filled lenses, I opened the WordPress editing platform for the Will Travel for Vegan Food website and updated one of the pages to reflect Nate's contributions to the trip. It was something I had been intending to do for a while—a long overdue request from Nate.

I'm not sure when I finally fell asleep that night, but it turned out that it would be the last time we'd ever speak.

'BANG, BANG, BANG, BANG!'

A stout, middle-aged man in a security guard uniform stood, one hand on his hip and the other cupped over his brow, peering into the passenger side window. I nearly fell backwards in panic and began retracing my steps. Had I parked in a handicapped spot? Did I need to pay for parking?

I quickly pulled on my grey "VEGAN" hoodie, fixed my hair back into a loose bun, and cleared my throat. I opened the divider curtains, went to the passenger door, sat down, and opened the door a few inches.

"Ma'am, were you sleeping in there?" said the man, with

an aggressive, deep Southern accent.

"Oh, well I didn't sleep here overnight. I just pulled in a little while ago," I said.

"That's not what I asked you, ma'am. Were you sleeping in your vehicle?" he asked.

"I just pulled in a few minutes ago and wasn't quite ready to start the day, so I was resting my eyes for a few minutes," I said.

"I'm going to have you arrested if you don't leave immediately," he replied. "I saw you pull in. You never got out of your vehicle and it's been two hours. If you're not going to patronize the establishments here then you need to go," he continued.

"I'm so sorry! I was planning to go to that Starbucks around 8:30," I said.

"If you don't leave right now, I'm going to have you arrested ma'am. You can't sleep here. Go now before I call the cops," he retorted, nearly yelling at this point.

Too tired and confused to continue the conversation—and having zero interest in being arrested for the first time—I kept one hand on the inside handle of the door and raised the other in submission.

"Okay. I'll leave," I said.

Before I shut the door fully, he threw in a final word: "If you're not gone in two minutes, I'm going to have you arrested."

I walked to the back of the van and opened the remaining curtains, grabbed my phone from the bed, and hustled into the driver's seat. 'Jug, jug, jug, jug' said the van in response to asking her to start. I closed my eyes and exhaled deeply. 'Jug, jug, cah-jug, vroom,' she started.

My red-framed glasses bumped up and down on my nose as I tucked my knuckles beneath them to rub away the morning's eye crusts.

I pressed my naked foot against the brake pedal, pulled the gear lever toward me, 'click, click, click, click,' until it landed atop the letter D; I lifted my foot, then placed it on the gas pedal. I looked up momentarily and scanned the vacant parking lot.

Not a single other vehicle in sight, except for the parking lot security guard's jeep that was creeping up behind Gerty's bumper.

As I drove toward the parking lot exit, it occurred to me that I hadn't acted with much caution when opening the door to this agitated stranger. What if he had been a burglar or murderer disguised as a security guard? No one else was around! As I heavily swallowed the scary what-if scenarios, I calmed at the idea of how it would, at the very least, make for an interesting blog post. He was, after all, just an unpleasant man with nothing better to do than his job.

part three

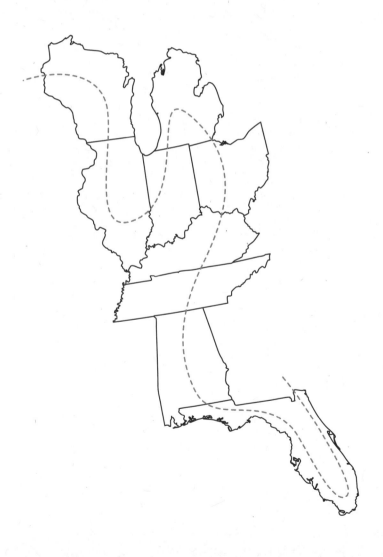

CHAPTER 10

IMPROVISATION

My internal emergency alarm hurled my body straight up at the waist, like an untethered seesaw, resulting in the immediate clocking of my forehead against the ceiling of the van. "Gah!" I whispered as I pressed a palm to my stinging brow.

Despite having lived in the van for several months now, I still somehow miscalculated the distance between my super comfy makeshift platform bed and the rectangular wood-paneled plastic light fixture directly above.

While waiting for my eyes to adjust, I dug around in the blankets, through the sleeping bag, and between the pillows in search of my phone.

It was six in the morning and my stomach was gurgling in such a way that I knew exactly what was coming.

"Gah," I said, louder this time, wrapping an arm around my waist.

"No, no, no this cannot be happening!" I hadn't account-ed for anything more than a 'number one' while in the van. Up until now, my method had worked well. During the days, I would be out and about—in restaurants to eat, and in in-ternet cafés or coffee shops to work—so there were plenty of

81

opportunities to manage number twos. But I quickly realized that I had little control over what was about to happen.

It was early May and the sun was already ablaze in St. Augustine, Florida. With very rare moments of stomach sensitivity in my adult years, I began to gather the evidence as to why my bowels demanded I wake up two hours earlier than normal. Then it hit me. Dinner.

Food poisoning? Nope. The culprit was an incredibly delicious, fully raw and therefore high-in-fiber meal that had churned its way down, down, down as I quietly slept the night away.

With another heavy gurgle, I snapped back into the present moment. Oh shit. Literally.

I had to go like never before, and it was on its way, despite my lack of preparedness. I started talking out loud, "Please just wait until I can find an open general store or coffeehouse." To which my bowels replied, "Oh, you're so silly. Just doing my job over here! Smiley face."

I scooted down the bed, like a dog with butt worms, and slowly stood while actively clenching as much as humanly possible. I desperately began searching the van for an answer. "What to do? What to do?" I looked down at my bare feet, and toed the dark green, 1970s-style carpeted floor that blanketed the only open space left in the van.

A few months earlier, Dad and Nate had removed Gerty's two rows of bucket seats and replaced them with a raised, wall-to-wall piece of plywood, which held the custom-sized mattress. The entire two-foot by four-foot space directly behind the driver's seat held a handmade wooden storage box that contained my clothes and some books.

I glanced at the double side doors to my right, as if they'd speak some magical words that would somehow resolve my need to GO. No sooner did I feel tiny beads of sweat form between my upper lip, on the bridge of my nose, and across my forehead. My whole body began to feel warm, while some-how also generating cold chills in second-by-second waves. I'd completely forgotten about the welt that was taking shape on my noggin as I literally took to holding my cheeks together in an effort to deter the increasingly insistent number two.

My mind raced between just giving in right then and there, crapping in the middle of the van, or jumping into the driver's seat in search of a public restroom.

Images of Golgothan chasing me down began flashing in my brain, as I feared that the simple act of sitting would trigger an undesirable response. I loved those Emerson sweatpants too much to let that happen! Then again, they were already brown anyway. Hmm.

As I tried to estimate how long it would take to drive back into the small touristy town, I noticed a mild discomfort in my neck. Even though I'm only five-foot-two, the carpeted area of the van was a hair too low, leaving my head tilted to one side. "Oh crap, oh crap," I said to myself as my stomach gurgled, audibly this time. I knew that if all I did was continue cussing out the different acceptable words for poop, I'd soon be scrubbing it out of the van's matted flooring.

'That backpack is kind of old; I could tip it over and empty it out right now, take a squat, then just throw it away. No, that won't work. What if someone tried to repurpose it? No, no, no.'

I picked up my phone, opened the Yelp! app, and searched for "coffee wifi." This one looks good, click—doesn't open until eight. Gah! How about this one—opens at seven. No! Rumble, growl, squeak. I couldn't hold out much longer. I leaned forward and quietly opened the double side doors to assess a possible quick disposal right there, on the side of the road, in the residential neighborhood. 'It won't take long, right? No one would see me; everyone is still sleeping, right?'

The night prior, following a delightful and, as it turned out, flattering dinner, I landed a great parking spot in front of a piece of property up for sale. It was across the street from one of the restaurant's employees, whom I met while dining at the bar that night. She assured me it was a quiet and safe neighborhood, and that no one would bother me. And to think, just twelve hours before this literally gut-wrenching moment, I was being wooed by a kind gentleman with the most stunning blue eyes and thick, black, tribal-like tattoos adorning his arms and neck.

It must have been the sassy way in which I was hunched over, sexily pointing my camera phone at a cup of chipotle kale soup. The sun was beginning to set, casting an awkward light within the restaurant, equal parts fluorescent and natural. Not the best for taking food photos, I'd learn. I held the phone horizontally, tapped the screen to select its focus, tilting it from this side to that, and tapped the screen again, until the angle and lighting was as pleasing as I could manage using an iPhone. I placed my thumb on the grey oblong shape, with an image of a tiny camera in the middle of it, notifying the application that I wished to take a photograph. With a single simulated click, the image was now stored in my phone's memory, ready for upload and sharing on my blog and Facebook page.

Since I was the only person seated at the bar, and being almost too aware of my surroundings at the time—still adjusting to the life of a solo female traveler—I was immediately and sharply aware of the sound of a neighboring barstool being sidled up next to me.

Taking note peripherally, I continued searching for the best angle and focus for my current soupy subject. Feeling a quick pulse of embarrassment, I captured one more still, and then pressed the silver sleep button on the top of my phone and set it down. Without directly looking his way, I noticed that he'd opened a book, shoulders angled open in my direction. For a moment, I felt relieved that perhaps he was just sitting nearby because that's what people do. We huddle; we're pack animals; we like to be near other beings.

I took a deep self-reassuring breath and placed the green cloth napkin on my lap, making sure to fold it in half, corner to corner, with the open seam facing toward me, just like I was taught during a grad school etiquette seminar.

"Every business professional should know how to properly conduct themselves during a dinner meeting or networking event," the instructor had said.

I picked up my spoon and properly pressed the back of it into the glossy orange substance, allowing the farthest edge of the utensil to tip slightly deeper, as I carefully watched its concave center fill with the chilled liquid.

"Can I read the first few paragraphs of this chapter aloud to you?" he asked as I lifted the spoon halfway to my mouth. I stopped and didn't move for what felt like 10 minutes—meerkat style. I continued, gracefully completing the motion, and carefully sipped up the spoonful. I quickly set down the spoon and reached for a glass of room temperature alkalized water.

"Oh my goodness, so spicy!" I brought the glass to my lips and turned to face him, tipping my chin slightly to meet his gaze.

The alarming contrast of his shattering crystal clear eyes against the jet-black ink that poured above the collar of his shirt and on up to the base of his chin caught me off guard. He had short, dark brown hair with natural waves that jutted out slightly over each ear.

I consciously kept my shoulders straight ahead, pointed toward the bar, displaying the intended briefness of our exchange. My forward-facing shoulders and tipped-chin reaction was practically involuntary, and it occurred to me that I was reenacting body language behavior I'd learned years earlier from Natural Horsemanship instructors. But I was doing it completely backwards. When seeking dominance or commanding attention, the horseman squares her shoulders directly at the horse. It's only when she welcomes the horse to approach that she would turn her shoulders and look away, avoiding eye contact all together. Was I inviting this intriguing stranger into my space or asserting my dominance? Or both?

"Sorry, what? Oh, uh, sure I guess," I blurted, thrown by his question. No one's ever offered to read to me before as a (presumed) method of flirtation.

"My name is Jesse, by the way" he said, followed with a broad, impressive smile.

"Hi. I'm Kristin," I said, extending my right arm to assert a formal business handshake.

Jesse went on to read page after page, describing the connection of tattoo artistry with religion history.

Admittedly, it was pretty interesting stuff, though I caught myself going in and out of moments where I stopped listening and was wholly focused on the tone of Jesse's voice, the movement of his lips, and the way the setting sunlight danced on his tattoos. I softened; we talked and ended up having a really nice dinner together. I also learned that Jesse's tattoo shop was nearby, so he was a frequent customer at Present Moment Café. He seemed to know the staff really well, and introduced me to the bartender, who ended up encouraging me to park across the street from her place—in the residential neighborhood where I would find myself the next morning, abruptly awakened by a rumbling stomach.

Baby wipes! A recent purchase to aid in the days-without-a-shower freshening-up routine (great for armpits!), I almost forgot I had them until I was on my knees desperately clinging to the final moments before I could no longer keep it together. Another quick rotation revealed a paper shopping bag from Native Sun Natural Foods Market. I had stopped in just a few days earlier to stock up on snacks for my coastal drive from Jacksonville.

This was it. I had to. Even if I *could* locate a public restroom, it was too late. I emptied the double-layered paper bag (I'm so grateful to the bagger who opted to double up, oh my goodness), tore the sides a little more than a quarter of the way down, and folded them over to create a splash guard of sorts. Oh my! I placed the baby wipes by my side, pulled down my sweatpants, and carefully balanced on my heels while holding the paper bag against my bum. Success!

Oh the relief! There are no words to describe how freeing that moment was. After being overly thorough with the baby wipes—and hand sanitizer, and disinfectant spray, which I kept for the occasional van-dwelling cleanse—I dropped the dirtied biodegradable cleaning supplies into the bag with the poo monster, closed it up, and disposed of it at the nearest dump.

CHAPTER 11

DEER RUN

With the driver's side window rolled down, I pressed the fingers of my left hand together, letting them glide along the gusty waves of the motion-driven wind that swept alongside the van. Atop the wave, below the wave. Atop the wave, below the wave, momentarily broken in sequence by the side mirror.

The east coast of Florida was behind me, but not long gone, as I headed south along the narrow seven-mile bridge on my way to the southernmost point of the continental United States.

My friend Ben would arrive at the Key West airport in a few hours, to join me for the West Coast portion of my Florida exploration, up through our one stop in Alabama, and a brief layover in his home base of Chattanooga, Tennessee, before I'd once again continue on by myself.

In this moment, however, I wished someone would take the wheel, as I found my mind wandering back to the freshly formed memories Florida had thus far supplied: my first tele-vised appearance, in Jacksonville; my first public talk—about the trip—before a live audience, in Cocoa Beach; a breathtaking, lifelong dream-come-true wild manatee sighting*, on Merritt

*Check out the video of the manatees I saw, on YouTube.com/wtfveganfood.

Island; my first wild alligator sightings, in Blue Springs Park; and, during a midnight stroll along Juno Beach in West Palm, stumbling upon massive leatherback sea turtles laying eggs, with attentive, head-lamp baring members of the Sea Turtle Conservancy quietly watching over the mommas and marking the nests so that beach goers would not disturb them the next morning.
Incredible. 'Is this really my life?' I thought.

I withdrew my surfing hand from its windy waves, and placed it on the steering wheel so that I could retrieve my phone. It sat propped up in one of the wooden slats located just behind the dashboard's cup holders. The designers of this Gerty model even thought to include single, extended cutouts within each cup holder, for a mug's handle, I presumed.

"Okay, so I've got Asheville—that chocolate cake from Plant, oh my gosh! Charlotte—how incredible were those garden latkes from Fern? Wow! And Chapel Hill, all to write about from North Carolina. In South Carolina, I stopped in Columbia and Mount Pleasant. There were Decatur, Sandy Springs, and Atlanta stops made in Georgia. What else…?" I spoke, into the Voice Memos app on my phone. "Right, and Indian Harbor Beach, Fort Lauderdale—oh my gosh those sliders from Sublime were amazing—Marathon, Miami, Orlando, Palm Beach Gardens. Ah, yes, Christopher's Kitchen was so delicious—Palm Harbor, and St. Augustine. Oh! I wonder if should share the poop story on the blog. Hmm. Maybe not. Oh, there's also West Palm Beach—eep! The crab cakes from Darbsters! Have mercy! Winter Park—ugh, best ice cream in the country at Café 118. Man. This is something else," I said, as I continued taking verbal notes as reference points for upcoming blog posts.

I woke myself up with a single, on-the-verge-of-snoring snort, and my ears pricked to the sound of the van humming, air conditioning still blasting on high. It was my turn to schlep to the front and shut her off for a few hours before it'd get unbearably hot again.

It was our second or third night in the Keys, and Ben and I were sweating through our clothes and into the mattress of the bed as our bodies fought to keep us cool against the angry, muggy late-May heat that persisted through all hours of the day and night. Daytime wasn't as bad though. We found respite in little shops, coffeehouses, restaurants, and the occasional swim.

Despite the heat, I was glad to be back. I'd been about one year earlier, during a short vacation with Joe, so I was already familiar with the vegan eats of Help Yourself, Sugar Apple, and The Café. Joe and I had toured The Hemingway House and Butterfly Conservatory, canoodled with the six-toed cats, watched protected chicken flocks cross roads, biked around; and snorkeled, body-boarded, and parasailed our time away. I remember thinking, 'I'd like to live in the Keys someday.' I'd volunteer at Help Yourself, with their down-to-earth and knowledgeable veggie-loving staff, get odd jobs on touristy sailboats, and stroll along the palm tree-lined streets dotted with bright flowers, hidden walkways, and historic buildings. Then again, that was before living out of a non-temperature-controlled vehicle was part of the equation.

Given the heat, Ben and I made short work of the vegan eateries, some window shopping, and pseudo bar hopping; and scoped out Mallory Square and the Land's End Village before eagerly making our way up to Big Pine Key for our much-awaited stay at one of the only vegan owned and operated bed and breakfasts in the country.

The pebbles and sandy gravel crunched beneath Gerty's tires and then kicked up, softly pinging against her undercarriage as Ben and I slowly rolled up to the gate of Deer Run Bed and Breakfast.

We were greeted by Harry, one of the B&B's co-founders and owners. "Welcome to Deer Run!" he said, motioning us forward through the entryway. "Come on in. Your parking spot is the 'Utopia' one—same as the name of your room. I'll follow you down the driveway and then show you around a bit."

It was early evening, the orange-kissed sun now positioned atop the trees, and the moon, peering out from behind some grey, dusty clouds, accompanied our stroll from the van to the walkway that wrapped around the bed and breakfast, and on to our ground-floor room.

"Here we are," said Harry. "I'll let you two settle in before stopping down in a bit to make sure you have everything you need," he said.

"Thank you!" Ben and I replied, in unison.

The screened-in patio door squawked as it closed behind us, just as a cool, salty ocean breeze swept through the wiry pinholes that we were now surrounded by. A rustling tree, just a few feet beyond the porch, caught my eye. I pushed my glasses up my nose and squinted for a better look.

"Huh. Ben!" I whispered. "It's a baby deer!"

A spotted fawn sat close to the base of a tiny, twisting tree. With her legs folded beneath her, she rested her jet-black, rubbery-looking nose square to the ground and closed her eyes.

"She's so tiny," I said. Just then an adult deer emerged from behind the baby and stood over her, ears quickly flicking forward and then back while the rest of her body remained still as a statue. She then lowered her head and began grooming the petite fawn along the neck and chin.

"You're here at a great time of year," said a voice from outside our room. It was Jennifer, the other half of the B&B duo. "These are known as Key Deer," she said. "They're a protected and indigenous species who roam the island freely. They enjoy hanging around the bed and breakfast, and come and go as they please. You're here just in time for baby season," said Jennifer.

"Oh, and I thought you might like to try a bottle of our wine," Jennifer said, as she opened the screen door, stepped in, and handed it to me.

"Wow, thanks so much!" I said.

"Make yourselves at home. Relax. Breakfast is served at 8:30 every morning. Just follow that stairway up to the dining area and we'll have everything ready with coffee, juice, and a meal for you and the other guests," she said. Jennifer hugged us and then went back upstairs where she and Harry lived year-round while maintaining and running the B&B.

"This is incredible," Ben said as he unlocked and then slid open the floor-to-ceiling glass door, causing the inner drapery to gently float open, revealing Utopia.

Surrounded by pink and key lime green walls, white wicker furnishings, and coral-colored bedding topped with kitschy, color-coordinated stuffed turtles and fish, this beachside oasis felt like childhood magic. With my backpack still strung over one shoulder and the bottle of wine in hand, I noticed a box that sat on a small table, opposite the bed.

"Huh. Ben. Cupcakes!" I exclaimed.

I set my pack down and scanned the room: composting and recycling bins, tropical-inspired and uplifting pictures and paintings, and artisan-crafted tile inlay tabletops.

I turned back to the cupcakes and took one out to Ben, who was setting snacks out on the porch table: hummus, guacamole, and salsa with some blue corn chips and two wine glasses, ready for filling. We spent the night snacking, drinking, and reminiscing about our happenstance meeting in Atlanta, just a few weeks earlier.

Ben was one of just a few people who had heard about my travels relatively early on. We had shared a few email exchanges, and he offered me a place to crash when my travels would eventually take me to Chattanooga. It just so happened that we met a bit earlier than planned, while I was eating my way through Atlanta. We hit it off and embarked on a short-lived romantic romp, before parting ways after this mini excursion. He was of the open-relationship nature. Scrappy, tattooed from head to toe, and kind, Ben taught me a bit more about the world of open relationships, even gifting me *The Ethical Slut* and *Sex at Dawn*.

Admittedly, I was intrigued and remained open to it, early on. There was just something awkward about sitting cozied up to Ben in bed, writing a blog post on my computer while he openly wooed other potential partners on his. It was an interesting experience to say the least, but ultimately would result in some insecurity, confusion, and separation between us. For now though, Ben's company was much appreciated, and we did make a formidable travel team.

The next morning, I felt like an actress in one of those Folgers coffee commercials — surprisingly sprite and, with my eyes still closed, smiling as my nose caught the gentle essence of freshly-pressed waffles.

Ben and I meandered up to the shared dining area: a screened-in porch with a large table, surrounded by six cozy seats. In the immediate corner sat a rustic cabinet, home to an adorable self-serve coffee station with clay mugs, nondairy milks and creamers, and organic sugars.

Martin and Hilary, a middle-aged couple on their annual vacation, had already settled in, sipping homemade pineapple smoothies Jennifer had made that morning.

"Good morning, you two," Jennifer said, as she appeared from the kitchen with one plate of waffles and another over-flowing with steaming biscuits. "Please help yourself and have as much as you'd like," she said.

"Whoa. This looks fantastic!" I said.

"Wow. Thank you, Jen," Ben added.

We spent the next hour chowing down. The bright plates and

complimentary crocheted placemats, and friendly conversation with the other guests and with Harry and Jennifer, paired with the quiet stillness that surrounded the B&B, made me feel like we were on an epic, cabin-esque tropical camping adventure.

Ben and I spent the rest of the day exploring the nearby vegan eats, and, at the suggestion of Jennifer and Harry, stopped for one of the scheduled tours at The Turtle Hospital. We learned about the seven species of turtles and how humans have driven most of them to near extinction with our boats, fishing lines and nets, garbage, and the now-illegal turtle soup industry. This sanctuary primarily rehabilitates turtles, regularly performing flipper amputations, and aiding turtles whose shells have been painfully detached from their bodies due to collisions with boat motors. Once detached, on any part of the turtles' bodies, they do not reconnect, leaving them with buoyancy issues that make it impossible for them to float properly for air or dive down to look for food. These turtles become lifelong members of the hospital since they can no longer fend for themselves in the wild. But, in most cases, turtles passing through the hospital are released back into the ocean once they're rehabbed.

On our second and final morning at Deer Run, Ben and I enjoyed fresh homemade chocolate chip muffins with a side of whole fruit, personal-sized frittata cups, and roasted potatoes for breakfast.

"Oh, yes, I think we've heard of your project before," said honeymooners Jocelyn and Meg. They had arrived at Deer Run the night before and joined Ben, Martin, Hilary, and me for breakfast.

"Oh, wow, that's so cool," I said. We chatted the morning away and then walked, full-bellied, back down to our room to pack up.

"You guys, before you go I'd love to show you around the grounds a bit more. You've got to see this septic system I'm working on," Harry said. We spent the next two hours or so learning the ins and outs of the ways Harry and Jennifer were going to incredible lengths to make their B&B as sustainable and eco-friendly as possible. We'd stop every few moments to silently watch the Key Deer pass by, nibble the grass, and groom each other, and—on a few rare occasions—get close enough that I thought I might even be able to pet one, though it was a prohibited gesture.

Just before climbing into the van, Jennifer ran out to us with a bag full of her homemade hummus, chopped vegetables for dipping, and her special cake donuts, "...to keep you from going hungry as you drive to your next destination," she said. After saying our final thank-you's, and admiring the dozens of impressive environmental and animal rights bumper stickers that embodied the tail of Jennifer's car, we embraced and said our goodbyes.

As we backed out of Utopia—the gravel and pebbles yet again crunching beneath Gerty's weight—I couldn't help but joyfully giggle to myself. With a bag full of snacks on my lap, and a dear friend in the pilot seat, I relaxed into the passenger-side headrest and closed my eyes. Filled with warmth from the conversations and kindness of new friends; being moved to tears by the passion that Jennifer and Harry so clearly embed into all they do for the B&B, its guests, and the Keys community; and realizing that this journey had only just begun.

Once Ben and I reached the Florida Panhandle, we drove about three hours north—from Pensacola to Montgomery, Alabama—to dine at a raw restaurant that afternoon. It was the one and only all-vegan restaurant I found in the entire state of Alabama.

The drive felt long. It was mid-June, and the sun was blazing hot. We were both pretty tired from our quick, five-day drive up the Florida coast, so you could say we were less than thrilled to find the restaurant closed when we arrived. I wasn't totally surprised though. It had been difficult to figure out their hours of operation, there was no phone number, and there was some association with a health and wellness center that I believed operated across the street. However, we somehow came to the conclusion that they were scheduled to be open when we arrived.

The entire street was eerily quiet as we parked, got out, and approached the front porch of the restaurant. It seemed to have been a home-turned-café. After knocking a few times, and peering into the windows to see if anyone was around, we decided to sit on the porch steps and pick at the leftovers we had from the night before.

A few minutes passed before a woman jogged toward us from across the street, and started asking us where we'd come from and if we'd heard the news. It didn't occur to me at first that she worked for the restaurant/health wellness facility until she said something like, "I'll get you some food, hold on." She unlocked the front door to the restaurant, went inside, and then emerged a few minutes later with two to-go containers full of food.

She went on to share that the neighborhood was on lock-down because there were some recent murders in the area, and the killer hadn't been caught yet.

"You two better get a move on. Everyone is staying in their homes, and it's probably best if you keep driving," she said.

Ben and I looked at each other and agreed with the now semi-frantic woman that we'd better leave right away.

"Drive safely now, y'hear," she said while pacing quickly back across the street.

We hopped in the van with our to-go containers and promptly continued on, to Chattanooga, Tennessee. Twenty and a half states down, twenty-seven and a half to go.

CHAPTER 12

TO HEAR THE MOVEMENTS

It was after 9PM on a Monday night. I pulled around the corner at 1st and West Fort Street, and parked illegally, putting Gerty's emergency flashers on. I was too tired and upset to keep driving. I had just hung up with my mom, and now all I could think about was the conversation I'd had with my grandfather over the phone a few weeks earlier. Besides, my new friend, Nicole, was going to call any minute with directions on where to park in relation to her apartment complex. We had never met before, only exchanged a handful of emails after she'd gotten wind of my expedition. She offered me a place to stay once I'd reached Detroit.

The phone startled me when it buzzed in my hand, the van still idling. "Hi, Kristin! It's Nicole. We're on our way from the gym. Where did you end up parking?"

Before I could bring myself to utter a single word I began to cry. This was my first phone conversation with Nicole, and I was so embarrassed that I first tried to hold in the sobs, until that seemed to cause them to double in size and volume.

"Hi," I said shakily.

"Is everything okay?" Nicole asked.

"I'm so sorry," I said, now through heaving breaths and heavy tears. "I just hung up with my mom, and I need to book a flight back to New York. It's my grandfather. He doesn't have much longer."

We hadn't yet hung up when Nicole and her partner, Chris, reached the van. It started raining through the humid night sky. She no sooner parked and flung her car door open, leaving it unclosed behind her, than she trotted up alongside the van.

It had been a few days since I'd last showered, it was hot, the air conditioner in the van had stopped working, and I was doubly sweaty from anxiety and sadness. I didn't want to hug her hello like I'd done with everyone else I'd met so far, because I didn't want her to see me crying or to catch my stink. But as I slid out of the van, nervous to even make soggy eye contact, she leaned in. We stood in the middle of the street and embraced warmly as our silhouettes cast out behind us, drawn forward by the headlights of her car, still running.

"Kris," said Mom. "Kris, are you there? I've got Pop on the phone for you."

She was calling from St. Mary's Hospital. I was surprised to hear they were at a hospital, since Pop had been living at the Eddy Heritage House Nursing & Rehab Center, and that's usually where she'd call from if I ever chatted with Pop over the phone. The Eddy—as Mom referred to it—was just a few miles from the house he'd built for my grandmother and their three kids, decades earlier, in Troy, New York.

He chose to move in a couple years after his wife, my Gram, started living there. Before he moved into the nursing home with Gram, he would take a senior citizens shuttle to and from their house to the nursing home, where he would spend all day by her side, seven days a week.

Gram had had a stroke nearly a decade earlier that, not long after, bound her to a wheelchair. Pop took care of her for a few years from their home with the assistance of a caregiver, who would stop in once a day to check on things. But, as his body slowed down, it became more difficult for him to lift her to and from bed, carry her to the bath, and prepare meals.

Stories of Gram's outgoing and adventuresome childhood, and strength and kindness as a mother, were never in short supply during family gatherings. Like the one about how as a teen she broke her leg after attempting to jump a barrel while ice-skating across a homemade pond. Or when, in her early sixties, she was diagnosed with colon cancer and, after the surgery that removed much of her large intestine, she was told she'd have to wear a colostomy bag outside of her body the rest of her life. Within a few months she fully recovered and overcame her diagnosis, remaining cancer- and colostomy bag-free for her remaining years.

Age, and perhaps a diet of too much chocolate—although it is hard to believe she liked chocolate more than I do—eventually caught up with her. The last few years of her life had taken away much of her memory, and her words. She rarely spoke at all, to anyone. I often wondered if she even recognized Mom after a while. My mother visited Gram every single day she spent in the home.

When Mom had called, I was sitting in the passenger seat of the van, parked in the u-shaped driveway of Good 'n' Raw, in Lakewood, Ohio. It was comfortably warm out that day, and I was about to dive into a small container of sunflower-based vegan tuna salad and a plate of raw nachos topped with hearty, walnut-based taco meat and a creamy cashew-based cheese sauce.

I could immediately tell by her tone and cracked words that things weren't good. Pop had been on a gradual decline for a few weeks now, but I suppose it's a thing that's, in many ways, impossible to prepare for.

"Hey, Mom. Yep, I'm here," I said. "Oh, okay. Put him on."

Pop was notoriously hard of hearing. His large-lobed Italian ears (decorated with grey and white bristly strands of hair, of varying sizes, jutting out from the inside and dancing along the top outer part of his ears too) would make you think they were designed for catching sound waves, no matter what. But over time, conversations turned into slowed-down shouting, so that he could make out what anyone was saying.

"HEY, POP. HOW ARE YOU?" I spoke, as loudly as I could without full-on yelling, into the tiny mic on my phone. I was glad to be inside the van, self-conscious of speaking so loudly.

"Kris? Kris, is that you?" he said, in a slow, muffled way.

"YES. IT'S KRIS. HI, POP!" I said.

"Oh, it's so good to hear your voice, Kris. Kris, how are you doing? Still traveling?"

"I'M WELL, POP. YES, STILL DRIVING AROUND THE COUNTRY."

"Oh, that's just wonderful, Kris. I'm so glad. Hey listen..." he said, and then he started to cry a little. "I, I just wanted to tell ya that I love ya. And that I'm proud of ya. I still love the way you were with Spirit. Gram and I loved going to your horse shows and watching you do those side steps and trail courses with that little pony of yours. You two were such a great team."

"I MISS THE HORSES, TOO, POP." I said, now trying to hold back my own tears.

"And..." he paused for a moment "...I wanted to say good-bye, Kris."

"OH. POP." And then I started to cry.

"I know my time is coming, and I just want you to know I love you and am so proud of you. You're wonderful. And Gram and I are so proud of ya."

"THANK YOU, POP. I LOVE YOU, TOO," I said.

He began to sniffle a bit more, and then Mom came back

on the phone. She was crying. "He's been calling everyone today, to say goodbye," she said.

Through his final days, my grandfather's mind was relatively sharp, but his body had been on the decline for several years. After Gram passed, about one year earlier, he started to go much quicker.

They were such a handsome couple, my grandparents. I always loved this one black-and-white photo of them, now browned and worn around the edges. Pop looked sharp, beaming with confidence in his army uniform, one leg propped up on the front bumper of a black car. Gram was standing next to the car, by one of the front tires. She was leaning against it, facing the camera; Pop was just behind and alongside her. Gram's hair was done up in 1950s-style waves, she had a big floppy hat on, and wore a beautiful but simple dress (pinched at the waist by a skinny belt), and saddle shoes. They looked happy.

This photo lived frameless atop their fireplace mantle along with dozens of other photos—some framed, others not—of Mom and her older brother and sister, and of me and my brother, and our cousins. My mom and aunt in their childhood baton twirling uniforms, my uncle in Boy Scout getups. Their own children's aging family photos, baby pictures, and dozens of their grandkids' school portraits.

In addition to the black-and-white one of them, there were two other photos—placed somewhat centered on the mantle— that always caught my eye whenever I'd scan the lineup.

The first was that of my mom in her late teens, sitting atop a large chestnut brown horse named Lady. Lady was mid-swishing her tail, her neck lowered to the side, scratching one of her forelegs. Mom looked ethereal—I'd rarely seen her as confident and happy as she appeared to be in that picture. She radiated contentedness and joy with her straight, waistlong brown hair pulled back into a loose, low ponytail. Her porcelain skin shone from her face like a beam of light, her sharp cheekbones glowed pink, and her deep green-blue eyes sparkled like Emerald City.

The other photo was of me with my pony, Spirit. We had won some blue and red ribbons at a local horse show that day. They were strung along the nearest rein, for the picture. I must have been 10 or so years old. My spindly, beige jodhpur-clad legs barely made it halfway down Spirit's hay-bellied sides, and my dome-shaped, black velvet helmet made me resemble a bobble-head, equestrian in nature.

Sometimes I'd look at that photo and feel as though time and space collapsed, that Scotty would beam me from present day to sometime circa 1992. My grandparents' living room would fade away, and streaks of light would zoom past me until I was no longer viewing the picture, but experiencing it as my pre-teen self—there on Spirit, holding the pose, waiting for Gram to snap the shot.

She'd say, "Kris. Kris, get her ears up. Jan [that's my mom], Jan will you get Spirit's ears up for the photo? Kris, smile. Show your teeth, smile!" she'd say, all while snapping away on her toy-looking camera, the thick strap of it slung around her neck.

Gram always had on a flowery blouse with either a pair of cotton, straight-legged blue pants, or a brown ankle-length skirt. She slept with curlers in almost every night, so her grey hair was perfectly curled into medium-sized swirls, every day.

"No, hold on, Kris. One more. Wait, let me get one more. Oh shoot, FRANK! HOW DO I PUT THE FLASH ON?" she'd shout to my grandfather. Photo taking was always a bit of a process with Pop and Gram; I loved every minute of it.

They never missed a single horse show, gymnastics showcase, school play, or dance recital. Not a single one. Their other grandkids lived in Virginia and Long Island; my brother and I were the closest to them, living in a small town just outside of Troy. They made it a point to show up, and be positive and supportive, no matter what my brother and I were into at the moment. I suspect that if my cousins had lived closer, they would have found a way to see all of us, as much as possible.

I never did grow out of my love for horses. It would become a largely defining element of my childhood, and Pop and Gram were fixtures at every event. Even once wheelchair-bound, my grandmother would insist on getting up early so that she and my grandfather could make it to the shows by 8AM, just in time for the first class. Friends and acquaintances, and regular show-goers, came to know my grandparents well. They had visitors at each show; no matter where along the ring they parked themselves, familiar faces would stop to chat, sometimes for hours at a time. Pop was the forever kind-hearted jokester, and Gram quietly carried a smile and a giggle that would warm your heart for days.

Nicole pulled back, and held me by the shoulders. Her cropped auburn hair cupped her head neatly. It stopped just below her ears—enough that she could just barely tuck it behind them. She was a bit taller than me, slender, and athletic-bodied. She had large, dark chocolate-brown eyes, deeper and more knowing than all the world's oceans.

"I'm so sorry. I, we just met, and I feel terrible that I'm a mess. And I smell…" I trailed off as she stood looking upon me like a gentle, concerned mother, and then picked up after me.

"Oh my gosh, no worries at all. It's okay. Everything will be okay."

She pulled me in for another hug before we determined that Gerty would remain in the private parking lot of her apartment complex, a large Double Tree Hotel that was half hotel, half Fort Shelby Tower Apartments.

I'd never met anyone like Nicole. Though I was beginning to open to the idea of what spirituality meant—intention setting, meditation, and energy healing—Nicole lived it. She manifested dream jobs and relationships and living situations. She found meaningful lessons in every life event, and I saw—for one of the first times in my life—what inner beauty looked like, on a complete stranger.

Here she was—she and her kind, dashingly tall, dark, wavy-haired, handsome boyfriend—taking in a smelly, crying, mess of a stranger who she met on the internet only a few months earlier. And yet she felt like a dear friend, like someone I'd known my whole life. We clicked. Though I went to bed early that first night—after taking a long, much needed shower—for my remaining days in Detroit we'd stay up talking about food, family, travel, and romance. We watched ridiculous YouTube videos into the wee hours of the night. She introduced me to her friends, we dined in and out together, and I truly felt cared for—without a hint of judgment or question.

One of my favorite meals was enjoyed at Nicole's living room table. We ordered nearly one of everything from Detroit Vegan Soul. Co-founders and owners Erika and Kirsten personally delivered our goodies, and Nicole's friend Kim joined us for the feast. The table overflowed with what—to this day—is the best soul food I've ever had the pleasure of enjoying. In tapas-style fashion, we passed compostable to-go containers around and across the table, scooping out hefty spoonfuls of the most tender collard greens and creamy mac 'n' cheese. We sliced the two large slabs of seitan steak with mashed taters doused in a thick, dark brown, home-style mushroom gravy sauce. There were crispy, fried spring rolls with sweet and sour dipping sauce, salty string beans, and mini corn muffins that crumbled delicately into our hands. We even cut an avocado-topped veggie burger—with the fluffiest of buns—into thirds. We finished the meal off with Detroit Vegan Soul's warm apple pie, oatmeal muffins, and chocolate chip cookies that were so good, a single bite was enough to paralyze me for more than a few seconds.

Afterwards, the three of us reclined in a food coma—guts aching with delight—and gabbed the rest of the day away, talking travel, relationships, marriage, and the universe. I could relive that meal, and Nicole and Kim's company, every day without tiring of it.

The day of my flight, Nicole handed me a paper bag that she'd packed full of snacks, then drove me to the airport so I could go home for Pop's funeral. She also picked me up when I returned to Detroit a week later. I learned that, while I was away, her dad had taken the van for a tune up and oil change, and replaced one of the non-working headlights.

It's no wonder this sweet young woman was so kind and generous—her family appeared to be equally so.

On the morning of my last day in Detroit, having returned from the funeral now and finishing up vegan food spotting, I sat tired and uncomfortable on a bar stool at Cacao Tree Café, eating a huge salad of baby spinach with cucumber, avocado, red cabbage, onions, carrots, sprouts, and house-dehydrated teriyaki almonds topped with ginger-lime dressing.

I schlepped back to the van, and discovered a parking ticket on Gerty's windshield. Apparently the meter was five minutes overdue. I left the parking ticket on the windshield, crawled into the van, rolled up into the blankets on the bed, and took a brief, deep nap. Afterwards, I plucked the parking ticket out from under the wiper, hopped into the driver's seat, filled out the ticket form, and put cash inside the envelope, before driving to the town police station to drop it off.

As I settled back into the driver's seat and buckled my seatbelt, I opened the Mail app on my phone for a quick scan, before heading out and on to Wisconsin. There was an email with the subject line: "Dear beautiful woman." It read:

> *You are stunning in the most epic way possible.*
> *I am so grateful for you!*
> *Tap Dancing to Hear the Movements,*
> *Nicole*

CHAPTER 13

SPIRIT LITTLEFOOT

Even from several yards away, my eight-year-old eyes could tell she was absolutely perfect. Too excited to be nervous and too anxious to be excited, I stammered to catch glimpses of her through the weathered, wooden split-rail fencing that separated us.

As Sandy, the farm manager, walked out to the field to retrieve the pony, my spindly legs paced double time back to the car to grab my helmet, its midnight-colored, velvety surface shielded by my favorite elastic zebra print cover. I had prepared at home several hours earlier, carefully laying out pintsized beige britches snazzily accented with matching zigzag stitching down each outer seam.

I peered at my brand new black rubber boots that noisily flapped forward and backward against my shins and narrow calves, squeaking in cadence to my short, erratic stride. I clicked the helmet strap into place, snug under my chin, just like my best friend Kaitlin had taught me to do two years earlier. I paused and thought, 'This could be it. She could be the one.'

My parents and I had spent that summer looking at a few different horses and ponies. This unnamed gentle, furry, round-bellied creature would be our first family member of the equine persuasion. I'd spent the previous two years in 4-H taking horse-back riding lessons with friends, and attending club meetings where we opened with the organization's pledge and discussed our goals for the year.

"I pledge my head to clearer thinking, my heart to greater loyalty, my hands to larger service, and my health to better living for my club, my community, my country, and my world." This intimate group, which my parents would later become leaders of and mentors to other new families, was known as The Happy Horsemen.

Despite being a quiet, scrawny, and introverted young lady with long, frizzy, mousy brown hair and feet so flat and pre-posterously long for my short stature that Dad often joked he'd never need to buy me real skis, I was determined at our monthly club meetings to push through the anxiety that lay dormant in the back of my throat. I would prove to my parents that I wanted a pony more than anything else in this world. I would be a horseman. Cue the *My Little Pony* theme song.

They called her The Little Bay Mare. She was smaller than most of the other horses on their property, standing 14-hands-tall at her withers, putting her in the large pony category. Her black points (the color of the mane, tail, and lower half of the legs) with a dark brown coat classified her as dark bay in color.

The Little Bay Mare entered the aisle of the barn that ran between what seemed like endless rows of stalls. Sandy latched a single flat—a 2-inch-wide and about 10-foot-long nylon tie—to each side of the mare's halter. I leaned against Mom and whispered to myself, "Those are called cross ties."

The lessons from 4-H were rapidly flashing before me. I wanted Sandy and the other seasoned horsemen at the farm to be aware of all the knowledge I'd acquired in the few years leading up to this moment, even though I'd been keeping the well trained thoughts to myself. 'Cross ties hang from a high point, usually well above even the tallest horse, attached to a sturdy, structural floor-to-ceiling support beam. A horse is walked up so that its head stops directly in the middle of the opposing ties. They are fitted loosely so that the horse can move her head comfortably, but are intended to keep her from wandering off during grooming.'

By this point, I'd logged hundreds of obsessive hours watching my friends work with their horses, listening to guest lecturers and instructors, studying pictures, and eventually even working my way up to one of the scariest annual 4-H activities: giving a publicly presented and judged demonstration about something I had learned that year. Crisp white poster boards, rulers, and colored markers soon became almost as common as my desire to vomit before every presentation.

Even though she too was only eight years old—making her closer to the equivalent of human teenage years—The Little Bay Mare already knew the cross ties routine. She stopped in exactly the right spot, tipped a hind hoof forward into resting position, and lowered to relax her head and neck as our gaze met for the first time.

My eyes moved to a little white patch of swirly fur that whirled out crazily in every direction, like a teeny bright solar system smack dab in the middle of her forehead. Her resting leg was marked with a partial coronet, meaning that there was white fur lining the coronary band, where the top of her hoof met the lowest part of her leg.

I moved closer and slowly lifted my hand to present an open palm to her muzzle. She stretched forward slightly and nuzzled around, breathing heavily into my hand. Warm and softer than I could have imagined, her muzzle had an almost cartoon-like pliability to it. Like a deceptively awkward elephant trunk, a horse's muzzle is one of its most critical

forms of communication, teeming with sensitivity and unbelievable strength.

In one giant exhale, she caused the hair that had fallen from
beneath my helmet to shuffle about wildly. A high-pitched
giggle escaped from my belly, which seemed to catch her off
guard as she suddenly and inquisitively raised her head and
neck, simultaneously pitching both ears forward in my direction. If I'd had the emotional capacity at the time, I probably
would have cried with joy for The Little Bay Mare and me;
we had an immediate connection. Soul sisters. That's what
we'd become.

My parents and I spent several hours at the farm that day,
where I practiced leading The Little Bay Mare around, riding
her with guidance from Sandy, and falling completely in love. It
had been only a few weeks prior when my itty-bitty voice swung
into full vibrato for one final tug at my parents' heartstrings
with an original rendition of "Somewhere Over The Rainbow."

"Somewhere out there, there's a horse for me…" This had
followed the devastating news that Cloud, a much taller white
horse I had my heart set on, passed away before we even had
a chance to say, "Yes, we'll take him."

Shortly after the "Somewhere Over The Rainbow" car ride,
my father noticed a horse farm on his way home from work one
afternoon. In perfectly executed, unfettered form, he turned
around and decided to ask if they happened to have any horses
for sale. The next weekend, I was palm to nose with The Little
Bay Mare and my parents were writing a check.

In a group effort, my older brother and I landed on a new
name for "the pone" (as Dad would grow to lovingly call her):
Spirit Littlefoot. I was particularly enchanted with her surname,
as it was inspired by my favorite character in the movie *The
Land Before Time*.

For the next eight years together—well before I found my
way to veganism and then to a deeper understanding of what

it means ethically to work with these magnificent creatures—Spirit and I would make a remarkable pair as we found our way to blue ribbons, plastic trophies, and championships at local and statewide horse shows and 4-H events.

When the time came for me to move up in level, Spirit and I would continue to work together to teach new aspiring horsemen the ins and outs of gentle horsemanship. By the time I was 16, Spirit and I were a team of a different kind, giving riding lessons in the backyard to children as young as three years old and to adults more than twice my age. Also, instead of attending house parties or going to other social events with classmates, I spent most nights and weekends in the barn with Spirit and the other horses.

At our maximum capacity, we had six horses in our modest backyard family farm. Some were our own; others were there for me to work with on behalf of their owners. But Spirit was the very first equine to step foot onto that land while we owned it. In fact, we purchased the house, which my parents are still in today, primarily so Spirit could live with us instead of at a friend's place.

Before long, my childhood love turned into a career focus. I went on to major in Business Management with a Specialization in Equestrian Studies at Cazenovia College in Central New York.

After college, I spent a couple years working in the equine industry, and then underwent a significant lifestyle change (moving to Boston for grad school) that facilitated my decision to change career paths, and ultimately moved me away from the magical world of equines.

Not only had I escaped the clutches of my sleepy hometown—a rural village populated by no more than 4000 people—and moved to the "the big city of Boston," as I'd joking remark to friends, but I also would become the first of my immediate family to obtain a bachelor's degree and then a master's degree.

Having grown up within a community that tended toward the idea that "everyone is out to get you, scam you, or hurt you," it definitely made dreaming big a bit of a challenge. Fortunately for my brother and me, our parents did not share the same insights of most of those around us. They always encouraged Josh and me to pursue our passions, and they did whatever they could to ensure we were well cared for, even if it meant spending beyond their means.

I think it was because Dad and Mom both grew up in households that struggled financially that they worked so hard to create a better life for our family.

College was only about three hours from home, situated in a town not much bigger than the one I was raised in. Even though I grew leaps and bounds as an independent and more free-thinking young adult while in college, it was my move to "the big city of Boston," paired with making new friends while in grad school—many of whom were international students—and more actively diving into the vegan community, that really lit me up, set me on a new path, and left me questioning if my life spent working with horses was more cruel than anything else. I wondered, 'Had I spent all of my childhood and early adult life *exploiting* these animals that I loved so much?'

All of this did not change the fact that absolutely everything about who I was, who I wanted to be, and who I am today is directly tied to Spirit; and that my entire childhood, teen, and early adult years centered around working with these beautiful, powerful, sensitive, and expressive creatures.

In a way, I feel as though I've lived two very different lives— the first half devoted fully to the nuances of horses, and the second defending them (and all other sentient beings) by way of the vegan movement. Two seemingly different worlds have gently intersected at one very important point: compassion.

Perhaps the joining of Spirit to our family was the first step in my journey towards veganism. I loved that pony fiercely and without hesitation; there was nothing I wouldn't do for her. The concept isn't really all that strange. Over 30% of US households have either cats or dogs, or both. Forming bonds with animals is in our DNA. So why should that logic apply to only a specific subset of species? I suppose that's the very question veganism poses to us all.

CHAPTER 14

LOCKPORT

As I drove away from Detroit, the thought of the incredibly unique and delicious cacao mocha latte from Great Lakes Coffee I had enjoyed a few days earlier held my thoughts captive. Mostly, I was thinking that I'd probably never have it again. Unless, of course, I found a reason to be back in Detroit. Though I suppose that's how the story goes for all of the amazing food, beverages, and people I fell in love with while on this grand adventure.

About that mocha—I held one end of the narrow four-inch, craft-store-like spindle of wood, swirling it clockwise around the teacup that held one shot of espresso and twelve ounces of steamed almond milk. On the other end of the spindle was a thick miniature monster truck tire-sized block of onyx-colored cacao. With each rotation of my wrist, the creamy milk darkened.

I'd occasionally lean the spindle on the edge of the cup, leaving the chunk of cacao set in the middle to keep melting, while I continued tapping away on my keyboard. I had been swiftly assembling a blog post about spending that year's 4th of July in Columbus, Ohio—marching in the Doo Dah Parade with "300 Vegans 4 Independence Day," and afterwards celebrating with fellow parade-goers at a vegan bar called Hal & Al's. The group indulged in root beer floats, eight-layer nacho plates, fried Oreos, fried pickles, pizza, bratwurst, fried avocados, and pretty much every veganized version of the best bar food.

As I continued heading southwest, it was getting close to dinnertime. I was nearing Chicago, en route from Detroit to Madison, Wisconsin. Since Nate and I had hit up every totally vegan establishment in Illinois those few months earlier, I didn't *need* to stop in, fighting the city's notoriously hectic rush-hour traffic. I did have a few snacks with me, but with my unanswered yearnings for a melty, cacao-based sweet drink paired with the realization that I was so very close to one of my all-time favorite restaurants in the entire country, I just had to stop.

'C'mon, Kristin. When will you be this close to Chicago again?' I asked myself.

The Chicago Diner was one of my first restaurant loves. I mean, I really *love* this place. The first time I dined here had been more than two years earlier. Joe and I were visiting his family and, being the type of person who—after becoming vegan—always scheduled her travel plans around a locale's restaurants, I'd had my eye on the Diner for quite some time.

Joe and I sat in one of the booths to the right of the entrance. We had spicy buffalo-breaded seitan wings with vegan ranch dipping sauce as an appetizer. At the recommendation of a friend, I ordered the Dagwood sandwich. It was made up of thinly-sliced roast beef- and corned beef-style seitan, strips of greasy vegan bacon and melted cashew-based cheese sauce, lettuce, tomato, onion, pepperoncini, and spicy pepper sauce all piled on a spongy baguette. This gem came with a side of sweet potato fries and a crisp dill pickle spear. I could only eat a third of it, but that didn't stop me from ordering dessert. For dessert, I slurped down a cookie dough peanut butter milkshake, mounted with swirls of coconut whipped cream that came to a point at the tippy top, dotted with sprinkled chocolate chips.

En route once again to the Diner, I drove up North Halsted in Boystown, and miraculously found a parking spot that accommodated Gerty's generous girth. It was a beautiful summer evening in late July, right around the time of year I first fell for the entire city of Chicago, which had been a few years earlier on an entirely separate excursion, with my dear friend Melis.

Melis was my best friend in grad school. We had gone on a few travel adventures during school breaks, like our week-long road trip from Vancouver to San Francisco, and our weekend getaway to Chicago, where we indulged in all the touristy stuff that Joe never wanted to do since he'd done them all a dozen times already.

I even got my first-ever tattoo that weekend in Chicago with Melis. I was so nervous that I almost backed out. I kept thinking about what Mom used to say for why she'd never get a tattoo: "Oh gosh. When I get old and senile, I worry that I'll forget that it's a tattoo and just scrub and scrub to try and remove the ink stain. I'll rub my skin raw, and I'll just panic that it won't come off!"

Come to think of it, I had lunch at The Chicago Diner just before getting that tattoo. Melis and I met up with Joe's sister for lunch that day, and then she walked us to a nearby tattoo parlor. The size of a cufflink, placed just below my left wrist bone, it took no more than 10 minutes. After what felt like a few tiny bee stings, there it was: the vegan "V," an international symbol for veganism.

Once inside the Diner's warm embrace, I asked if I could sit on the back patio. It was beautiful out, and unusually quiet for the Diner. Having already taken detailed notes about previous meals from the Diner, I sat lightly into the green plastic patio chair, and sighed with great relief that I wouldn't have to stop every few bites to take notes. I did, however, pause to snap a few photos of my meal—to share on Facebook, Instagram, and Twitter, of course.

On this night, I opted for my absolute favorite of the Diner's meals: their country fried steak. It's this huge filet of battered and deep-fried seitan, served with the creamiest whipped mashed potatoes, and a side of sautéed veggies. That night's veggies were buttery broccoli, carrots, and zucchini.

My favorite method of indulging in this dish is to fork up a small mound of taters, layer that with a piece of one of the veggies, and then add a penny-sized portion of the seitan—a shish kebab version of the dish, if you will, a little bit of every-thing in one excruciatingly delicious forkful. With every bite, I'd hear Jesse Katsopolis in my ear: "Have mercy!"

While contemplating whether or not I could muster room for a milkshake, I started getting goose bumps at the rec-ollection of a conversation Nate and I once had with the founder and owner of a not-for-profit raw café in Lockport, Illinois. It was the last on our list of restaurants to visit in the state. They were relatively new when we stopped in about five months earlier, open only 11 months. I wondered how they were doing.

"So, I'm just going to set this here," I said, placing my phone in the center of the table, with the Voice Memos app recording.

"Okay, sounds good," said Laurie.

"Why don't you tell us your name again, and a bit about how the restaurant got started," I said.

A whimsical cover—certainly better than my own eight-year-old version—of "Somewhere Over the Rainbow" played softly through the restaurant's sound system. Nate, Laurie, and I sat close around a pear-shaped, sea foam green table, accented by a stroke of purple paint down the center that followed the shape of the table, with three purple dots along one side, resembling an artsy leaf.

It was winter at the time, and so I had on my favorite pair of black skinny jeans, with white knee-high socks and light brown, faux-leather knee-high boots. They were made by Steve Madden, but I had purchased them from Sudo Shoes, a cruelty-free shoe store in Cambridge, Massachusetts some time earlier. They weren't necessarily designed for winter wear; they just happened to look the part.

"Sure. My name is Laurie Sloan, and I'm the founder of Thanks Jordan Café, here in Lockport, Illinois," Laurie said.

I was immediately captivated by Laurie's piercing, powder blue eyes and her thick, dirty blonde locks. She was tall and looked fit. While we sat together, within a span of about 20 minutes, at least a half a dozen people stopped to say hello and give her a hug. Her phone buzzed every few minutes with important business calls. She was scattered yet focused somehow, busy yet keeping it all together in what seemed like an effortless and comfortable manner.

I had emailed Laurie—via a contact form on the Café's website—a few weeks earlier to inquire about meeting up with someone who could tell us more about the Café. I had no idea that we'd be meeting with the founder, or of the story she was about to tell us.

"The idea for a restaurant of some kind had been brewing for about twelve years, when I was first diagnosed with cancer. The last three years of which I had reached stage four," she said.

Nate and I sat attentively, nodding quietly as she continued.

"I've done everything in existence to help treat the cancer. You name it, I've tried it. And after going into remission the first time, I decided that I would eat real healthy, so if the cancer came back I could fight it.

"But I only kept getting sicker and sicker. Meanwhile, I was working out more, eating lots of what I thought were healthy foods, and I still got more and more sick. I couldn't understand it. Before and during some of my diagnosis, I was an ultra-marathoner—running up to 50 miles a day during training. I thought I was living in a healthy way.

"Around the same time, I had been coaching a running program for a leukemia and cancer society; and I wanted to bring that to my local community, so that I could give back and help others who were sick here too. My mom—who had always been good with money and was even named the very first female president of a bank—was retiring. She said, 'I'm inspired by everything you're doing, and your treatments; let's do this foundation together!'" Laurie said.

"After a couple of years of planning, we filed for a 501(c) (3). We planned to have the establishment run entirely by volunteers, and proceeds would go to benefit the Thanks Jordan Foundation.

"We got mail back approving the nonprofit status..." Laurie said. Then she stopped for a moment, and seemed to look past us. Her eyes shifted down to her clasped hands, elbows resting on the table. She moved to sit back in her chair, pulling her arms and hands down into her lap.

She took a breath, looked up and met my gaze, and said, "My mom was suddenly diagnosed with the same cancer I had been battling. She died six months later."

I wanted to glance over at Nate, but Laurie had my eyes on lockdown, both of us now welling up a little. I wanted to move closer, or hug her, but I could tell she had more to say, and I was on pins and needles. I felt like any movement—even a subtle one—would disturb the moment. My heart picked up a tick, and I could hear Nate's breathing pattern change a little. He too was feeling the emotion rise at the table.

Laurie continued: "So, I have this nonprofit in my name, my best friend in the world has just passed away, and then two months after that I was re-diagnosed with cancer. Then I had every reason inside me to do this and make a difference. So, I quit my job three years ago and went full-on to start Thanks Jordan Café."

I sat there, wondering how this woman in front of me appeared to be so vibrant, happy, and healthy considering all she'd been through. We each took a breath, and I finally broke to look over at Nate. We both seemed to be wearing faces of concern and sadness.

"But, it's not all sad," Laurie said. "So, I'm about a year into this project, pulling all the pieces together by myself, feeling totally lost and overwhelmed, and not physically getting any better. But I kept seeing this car around town, with a booming bumper sticker that read, 'Doin' it raw.' And I'm like, alright, this is someone I clearly need to know, because how many vegans live in this small town?

"So one day, I see this car at a gas station. I pulled up behind it and caught the woman as she was coming out to the car. I said, 'Don't think I'm crazy, but, I've got this not-for-profit in town and I'm thinking about doing this raw thing and taking my life and the Café in a new direction.' Before I could continue on, the woman said, 'Are you Laurie Sloan?'"

"Huh," Nate said, now sitting more forward on his seat, leaning onto the table with one elbow, bearded chin propped atop his hand.

"Then she said, 'You know what, I stopped at your store the other day, and I just felt like this is such a cool place and that I really must be part of it.'

"I said, 'Really?' and then she said, 'Yeah, in fact I'm going in tonight for my first training.'

"'That's amazing! My staff told me I'm training someone tonight! It must be you!'

"So then we spent the whole night talking about raw foods and my journey, while I trained her on some of the inner workings of the Café," Laurie told us.

And just when I thought Laurie's story had reached its finale—how the two women came together to refine what's now the fully-raw, volunteer-based nonprofit Café—she told us about where she currently stands on her battle with cancer.

"Shortly after meeting my now-business partner, I was diagnosed with cancer for the fourth time. This time it was non-Hodgkin's lymphoma. Turns out, it's a cancer caused by common cancer-fighting medical treatments. Go figure!

"After doing more research, I decided to take my health into my own hands—beyond what I had been doing already, in addition to chemo and all the other in-hospital treatments. So, I opted for the Gerson Therapy method. I kid you not, four days later, I felt better than I had in over a decade. Two months into my new regime, I went to see the same doctor who had been treating me since I was first diagnosed way back when. And get this: all of my numbers were cut in half! It was the first time in twelve years that my body responded to anything!

"The crazy thing is, instead of being supportive of this new way of treating my body—that was actually working to put the cancer into remission—my doctor up and fired me as a patient since I was no longer willing to follow his protocols. And you know what? I haven't been back since. I feel great, so why torture myself with MRIs and all these tests?"

"That's incredible," I said, before exhaling deeply, goose bumps still present.

"Yeah," Laurie said, "and all the money that's collected here at Thanks Jordan Café goes to three places: helping humans, promoting organic plant-based foods, and to animal welfare. That's it."

"I love it," I said, while reaching for my phone, and tapping the round, red 'stop' icon on the Voice Memos app.

Back at the Diner, I got a milkshake to-go, paid the bill, and began walking back to the van. It seemed as though my body was on autopilot, taking me to Gerty while my mind still traced over Laurie's story.

In the moment that I was sitting with her that day, I didn't understand why my body reacted the way it did—the goose bumps and cold chills when she revealed the death of her mother, or how far she'd come in treating herself solely with genuine nutrition. And then it occurred to me that it wasn't just a tale of woe, or of action. It wasn't just someone doing good in the world and living life to its fullest. It was of someone who—despite repeated and torturous obstacles—gave herself permission to care not only for others, but also for herself, during impossible times.

It makes me think of a quote by Aung San Suu Kyi that states: "If you're feeling helpless, help someone."

Though my journey hadn't touched the kind of heartache and bodily trauma that Laurie's had, I finally understood why I felt so moved by her story. To me, she represents strength, compassion, and a tenacity for life that few are capable of. Laurie made me a better person that day by demonstrating the qualities that I, too, wish to possess.

Whenever I think of her, or her nonprofit, or her mom, or her cancer, I will be strong, I will be compassionate, and I will give myself permission to move through this life with tenacious valor.

part four

CHAPTER 15

TEXICORN

"You ready for this?" he asked.

"Yep," I muffled through a clenched jaw, from beneath my left arm. It was hard to talk, and sort of hard to breathe in this position—lying there on my right side, facing him. My shirt was pulled halfway down, but a single piece of clear tape held a bit of it up slightly, just enough to conceal my chest.

I had spent the previous four weeks exploring Wisconsin, Missouri, Arkansas, Louisiana, and southern Texas. Now, it was after 10PM on a Friday night, and I found myself sobering up while under the needle of my friend Kristan's favorite Austin-area tattoo artist. As the artist slowly carved fresh ink into the tender flesh just below my left armpit, I aimed to focus all my thoughts and energy on happy memories from previous travels, or anything else really.

What I'd have given to be cozied up in one of those big squishy chairs at Mud Pie Vegan Bakery & Coffeehouse in Kansas City right then. The smell of chocolate chip cookies baking, the front case overflowing with muffins, rolls, pies, cakes, crumbly biscuits, and savory scones. I'd curl up, knees bent to the side, feet tucked snuggly to my tush, and use a throw pillow to help steady my computer perched atop my lap. I'd have a mug of a frothy soy mocha latte cupped in my hands. That coffeehouse was my absolute favorite thing about Missouri.

"OH. YUP. THAT'S A GOOD SPOT," I said with a raised voice, followed by a forced giggle, as the artist ran the needle across a particularly sensitive part. It's a funny thing about getting tattooed—sometimes I just can't tell where the needle is exactly, even when I feel sharpness or the acute burning sensation. But, during the sessions, I'd come to know the general area of those tender spots well when—over and over again—the needles would pass, pressing the ink permanently into the dermis layer of my skin.

Even though the lower armpit, upper ribcage area isn't a pleasant location for receiving millions of holes poked into one's skin, at this point I was officially no stranger to tattoos. Not like my brother, though, whose arms and legs are covered from top to bottom, with additional ink trailing the sides of his neck, the tops of his hands, and both sets of knuckles.

But there was this one time I was in Louisville, Kentucky, a few months back that I finally broke the 'I'll only ever have this one little tattoo on my wrist' deal I'd made with myself, since getting that vegan "V" way back when in Chicago.

Actually, I blame Twitter.

"I require at least three more tattoos in order to fit in here ;) @highlandcoffee #Louisville #vegantreats," I tweeted innocently enough one afternoon, while enjoying the teensiest, most delicious, creamy, peanut butter-topped cheesecake-like chocolate treat from Highland Coffee, on Bardstown Road.

Less than a minute later, my phone buzzed. It was the Hoot-Suite app notifying me that I had received a new tweet from @TattooCharlies. It read: "@wtfveganfood We can help! :) 39 years of quality in Louisville, cruelty free inks too! No animal ingredients or testing."

I sat, phone in hand, my mini chocolate cheesecake thing half gone, and was utterly thrilled. Not because someone replied to the note I had sent out via the Twitterverse, but because I go giggly over businesses that use social media in such a way that truly benefits their work. It's free advertising, free marketing, and free promotion for non- and for-profits, big and small. It levels the playing field, and it rocks my world when a company embraces it, pays attention, and appears to truly care. And that's exactly what Tattoo Charlie's did.

They not only replied to the tweet I sent out, but also used keywords that spoke directly to me: tattoos, quality, and cru-elty-free. This means they, at the very least, checked out my profile, and likely clicked through to my website to learn a little bit about me. This seemingly small effort goes a long way. Especially when you've just reached out to someone who is building her career around strategic marketing and social media consulting, and enjoys spending her free time reading business and marketing books, blogs, and watching hours of training videos on related subjects.

At that point, I was nearing the end of my stay in Louisville and, despite having considered getting a new tattoo while there, I hadn't committed to a shop, or even a design that I wanted. But this one tweet from Tattoo Charlie's impressed me so much that I made it a point to get a piece by them before leaving the city.

I walked into the shop the next day wearing my favorite dark grey t-shirt from the Herbivore Clothing Company. It had a largish, cute, bouncy, balloon-shaped elephant on the chest, accompanied by the words, "I'm vegan and I love you.

Dave, my assigned artist, had drawn up a rearing horse after—in a series of confusing emails wherein I had a new idea or style each time—I expressed an interest in getting something that represented my history with and love of horses. But it didn't feel right.

I looked down at my shirt. "How about this elephant?" I said, holding the bottom of my shirt out away from my body to flatten the image.

"Sure. We could do that for you," said Dave. "And if you still want a horse-related piece, I could draw up a small horseshoe."

"Sure. Sounds great!" I replied.

I shimmied myself into the squeaky plastic chair, and placed my right forearm on its armrest. I was a little nervous, but also excited since this would be my first more visible tattoo.

After chatting about placement, Dave set up his station, printed out the agreed-upon size of the elephant drawing, wiped my forearm with disinfectant, and set the outline onto my skin with stencil transfer paper. It took but 20 minutes, one curve at a time, permanently pressing the elephant into my skin. Dave then wiped the little ellie clean, and covered it with a bit of plastic, adhered with what looked like narrow strips of surgical tape.

My first super visible tattoo was installed. It felt like a terrifying victory of sorts. It would never come off, but it would probably look cool for a while.

We then repeated the process on my outer right wrist, matching the tiny horseshoe outline—accented by three tiny nail holes along each side—with the size of the vegan "V." Now, when I rest both hands under my chin, next to one another, it appears as though I own a pair of permanent mismatched cufflinks.

And then there was the time, a few months back, in Columbus, when I met a fellow vegan with a gorgeous, realistic animal tattoo. I asked who the artist was, and immediately became enthralled with his work. I emailed the artist that day to schedule an appointment. The piece became what's now the head and neck of a realistic zebra, nestled inside a picture frame, which lives on my right mid-to-lower ribcage. It took about three and a half hours to set the outline and some shading into place. Now *that* was a type of pain I can hardly put into words. It was so bad I nearly passed out the first time I tried to clean the beautifully painful thing. Thankfully, I was at a friend's place that night. I called her in, worried that I had become so dizzy from touching the burning, raised flesh that was howling in pain at the slightest touch. She helped me sit on the edge of the tub until I regained my bearings.

Keeping the piece clean in general became an interesting game while on the road. Since I had to clean it twice a day for at least two weeks, I ended up inventing a public restroom routine that seemed to do the trick.

I'd find a coffee shop that I wanted to work out of for the day, or freshen up at in the morning. I'd scope out the spot to be sure they had nondairy mocha mixes and milks, and then check the bathrooms for a single or family style one—the kind without stalls. Then, I'd go back to the van, grab my Stay True Organics Tattoo Aftercare, and throw a full body towel into my pack. Before settling in to do work I'd go to the restroom, take off all my clothes, and wrap the towel snug around my hips. Then I'd cup handfuls of tepid water and let it run down over the art. I'd wash it like that too, gently easing the slippery scrub on, and swirl it around until it became sudsy, before delicately running more water down to rinse it off. I'd then wave my hands frantically at the art to air-dry it, as I wasn't supposed to wipe it at all.

There was a time or two I didn't have a choice but to clean it in a bigger restroom with others coming in and out of the shared sink space. In those instances, I of course just lifted my shirt and tucked it into itself, to keep most of my top covered. But I did avoid eye contact, out of embarrassment and general awkwardness.

Bzzzzzz! Bzz! Bzzzz! 'This feels lovely. This is my joy!' I told myself.

"You doin' alright?" asked the Austin artist, speaking loudly over the dentist-drill-like sound of the tattoo machine.

"Mmmhmmm," I murmured.

I closed my eyes and thought back now to New Orleans. I had only spent three days in that beautiful bustling city, but it was one of my favorite stops to date.

"New York native Kristin Lajeunesse will travel for vegan food. In search of a lifestyle of self-discovery and non-conformity, Kristin quit her job and hit the road with the intention of visiting all 50 states while spreading her message of the significance of a cruelty-free, plant-based diet. Kristin, welcome to Louisiana Eats."

It was the morning after I'd arrived in The Big Easy. I was in a somewhat small padded room, with a large orange, foam-covered microphone an inch from my nose. It hung from an upside down L-shaped hinge. I had on black, pilot-sized headphones, and was being interviewed by local foodie Poppy Tooker on her popular radio show, *Louisiana Eats.*

Poppy's deep, raspy voice made me think of a sultry smoke-lounge singer from the 1960s. Her glossy grey hair was pulled taut into a high twist, held snug by a large beret.

It was my first radio interview of the trip so far, and I was nervous as all get out. Thanks to the conditioning of the show ring, my nerves almost always work *for* me. I'd go so far as to say that I even began to thrive on them in certain occasions— like out on the dance floor, or just before stepping in front of a crowd of strangers to give a presentation. There's something I love about that natural, anxiety-ridden high.

The night before my interview with Ms. Tooker, I stopped for dinner at the only completely vegan establishment in the entire state of Louisiana: The Wandering Buddha. Set on a small lattice-covered patio behind a bar, it was an order at the window, and choose your own seat, arrangement. The seating area was surrounded by greenery—tall trees whose branches hung low, and ivy that twisted in and out of the fencing. I decided it was quaint and perfect.

There were two couples seated at the remaining tables. Both were deeply engaged in conversations with their respective dates. I might have otherwise felt a ping of envy, being the only solo diner on this beautiful starry night. But with the excitement of exploring a brand new city, thinking about my interview with Poppy the next morning, and the insistent mosquitoes providing their own bit of distraction, I was glad to be alone. And I was glad that I *felt* glad about that fact.

I was first presented with a large, round plate half covered in what looked like two layers of pizza slices—four on top and four on the bottom. They turned out to be crunchy, rice pancake-like vegetable latkes with a delicate sweet dipping sauce. I had only finished half of one slice before the server brought out another large plate. In the center sat a perfectly round scoop of crisp white rice, sprinkled with black sesame seeds. The rice was accompanied by four pieces of seared tofu covered in a rich, sweet barbecue-esque sauce, and three different sautéed vegetable sides, each with varying levels of spiciness.

I had counted earlier that day, and so far I'd eaten at 250 restaurants since starting the trip. And yet this was quickly becoming, by far, one of my favorite meals. So much flavor was packed in these impeccable dishes, I could hardly fathom how it was possible to make food so delicious. I suppose that's why I've always been better at eating than at cooking.

"I believe that if you can reach someone through their stomach, compassion is just around the corner," said Christian, one of the restaurant co-owners. He sat with me for a moment that night to talk about my travels and his passion for his work. Clearer than Caribbean waters, Christian's passion radiated, through both his words as well as his food.

After the interview with Poppy, I strolled through the French Market, plucking from a basket of vegan jambalaya purchased at one of the food stalls there. Then, with my trusty black-and-red backpack in tow, I scouted Bourbon Street for a coffee shop to work out of for a bit.

I wandered into Gallery Burguieres, a beautiful art gallery filled with thick-lined, inspired, and unique drawings of zebras, giraffes, elephants, and colorful swirls and dips and shapes of all kinds. It turned out that the young artist and gallery owner, Ally, was a fellow vegan. We chatted for a while before I continued on.

Later that night, I made it through only four spoonfuls of a soupy, rather bland, rice and vegetable dish—the only vegan "gumbo" dish I could find in NOLA. I dropped some cash on the small window-seat table for two, in the large restaurant with a line out the door, and decided to try somewhere else.

I stepped out onto the busy sidewalk and suddenly remembered hearing about a great Vietnamese restaurant with a couple vegan dishes. I stood on the corner of Chartres and Peters Streets, scanning the Yelp! app. Magasin Vietnamese Café appeared at the top of the list with four out of five stars, and multiple reviews raving about their vegan Pho. With little time left before my scheduled Reverend Zombie's Voodoo Shop Guided Ghost Tour, I decided to give it a go.

"Did you really drive all the way from New York to Louisiana in that van, miss?" an older gentleman asked, keenly eyeing Gerty's license plate. He sat on a lawn chair on the sidewalk, and had been watching me park the van just there.

"I sure did!" I said, just before skipping across the street.

"Wooo Eeeee. That's a long drive, lady," said the man.

"It wasn't so bad," I shouted back, with a buoyed laugh.

"Have a good one!" I added, before opening the door to the restaurant.

Seated at a bar stool overlooking the street and its passersby, it was just beginning to get dark out as I carefully slurped the hot Pho broth from its native soup spoon while stirring the rice noodles and veggies around with chopsticks in my other hand. I'd grown to love Pho almost more than any other dish—the combination of the crunchy vegetables and their rice noodles soaking in salty, beige broth, the sides of sprouts and mint leaves, sweet and spicy sauces, and fresh lime to squeeze in. It's so involved that I must pay full attention to each meaningful scoop, swirl, and sip. Everything about consuming Pho is delightful, and makes me feel like a fancy food critic.

One of my favorite things about New Orleans is its sudden rain showers. One moment it'll be sunny and cloud-less, the next it will start raining so hard I half expect to see an alligator float by, like something out of *Jumanji*.

The day I was preparing to leave NOLA, I swung by Hey! Café to grab a few snacks and a mocha latte for the road. On my walk back to the van, I experienced one of those rapid rain showers. It was so warm and sunny out beforehand I hadn't thought to carry an umbrella. I ran for cover beneath the awning of a nearby house and pressed my back into the tan-colored siding, nearly overturning a green trash barrel embossed with a beautiful white fleur-de-lis.

A few cars splashed by, and a man ran in the opposite direction, crouched low, holding a newspaper over his head. Someone once compared the sound of rain to emptying a bag of M&M's slowly from one hand to the other. I momentarily closed my eyes and imagined the drops turning into a vegan version of those chocolaty treats. How sweet it is.

After about three minutes, I decided I'd make a beeline for the van, which was parked just a couple blocks away. As soon as I reached it and leapt inside, the rain began to subside and the sun almost immediately shown bright again. Nonetheless, I was soaked to the bone.

I was wearing flip-flops and one of my favorite summer dresses, now dripping at the hem. I changed into dry clothes and nestled into the driver's seat, braced for the haul to Houston, Texas.

Still giddy over the rain—the intensity and brevity of which I'd never really seen before—I placed my hands on the steering wheel and leaned forward to look up at the bright blue sky, to soak it in once more before moving on. A red, auburn, pink, yellow, and purple display of flower petals had fallen from the tree above onto Gerty's windshield. I began to well up at the clump of colorful petals, balanced on droplets of water left behind. I thought to myself, 'We are all *exactly* where we need to be.'

———

I had only met Kristan a couple of days before we decided to get matching tattoos. She had recently moved to Austin for work, and had heard about the road trip after seeing Ben and me at Sluggo's in Pensacola a few months back. I had left behind a "Will Travel for Vegan Food was here" window decal, some bumper stickers, and business cards. She picked up one of the bumper stickers, looked up the project online, and reached out. It just so happened that we both landed in Austin around the same time, so we met up for food, and then drinks, and then tattoos.

"It looks really good," Kristan said to me, standing behind the tattoo artist as he wiped the finished piece clean before covering it up.

"You're next!" I said. Kristan took my place on the flat, cushioned table while the artist prepped his station a second time.

I stood beside Craig, my other new friend—with whom I had stayed while traveling through Houston—who was in Austin playing a show with his band that weekend. The design we settled on was Craig's idea. And, in fact, he ended up getting the same piece, on his forearm, two days later.

"My friend created this design for a t-shirt line," Craig said, during a discussion that was going nowhere about what our matching ink should be. "Yeah, it's an outline of a unicorn rearing up, inside of the state of Texas. It's called a Texicorn," he said, while holding up an image of it displayed on his phone.

Kristan and I looked at each other, lit up, and shouted in unison: "TEXICOOOOORN!"

CHAPTER 16

HOW STUFF WORKS

I sat uneasily in the brown plastic chair at a Meineke in Tulsa, Oklahoma, during one of Gerty's regular tune-ups. Since we covered so much ground together, it was imperative for me to keep up on her oil changes and general maintenance. At about 11 months into the journey, I was preparing to head north into Kansas, Nebraska, and South Dakota. Therefore, I wanted to be sure she was tiptop, since I was expecting to drive through some new terrain, and have fewer resources at my disposal along the way.

A middle-aged woman was in the waiting area as well. She kept looking at me. I didn't blame her though, as I was coughing loudly and violently every minute or so.

With my immune system being constantly taxed by the continuous change of environment, sleepless nights, and eating everything and anything—as long as it was vegan—since the trip's beginning, it's no wonder I'd caught a cold a few weeks earlier. It was while I was in Houston. I woke up one morning with a fever, chills, sore throat, and full-body muscle soreness that lasted for about three days. Once the worst part of the sickness had passed, I soon developed a dry, uncontrollable cough. I'd get these tickles in the back of my throat, every other minute or so, that caused me to cough loudly and violently at times. It soon became difficult to eat or sleep, and my throat became painfully irritated and sore.

"How long have you had that cough?" the woman asked, her chair squeaking as she leaned toward me slightly.

"Going on three weeks," I replied.

"You know, I had something just like that last year around this time. I couldn't shake it for anything, so I went to my doctor and got some prescription cough syrup. Cleared it right up," she said.

"Thanks," I said, with a smile and then lunged forward holding my left ribcage to prepare for the impossible pain that had accompanied each excruciating cough.

I'd stopped noticing how sore my throat had gotten after one particularly violent cough that sent a jolt of pain so strong, up my left side. I thought for sure someone had sliced me clean from the base of my ribcage up and out through the collarbone. Just like when Arnold rips the T1000 nearly in half with a metal pole. But unlike the liquid metal machine, I couldn't just strong-arm the thing out of my body.

"You should get that checked out. Did you pull a muscle or something?" said the woman.

"I think so. It hurts like the devil just to sit here, or lie down, or breathe, or do anything really," I said.

"Yeah, well if you're not from around here, you could go to one of those walk-in clinics. There's a good one nearby with a pharmacy attached to it. It's pretty affordable, too," she said.

"I was trying to wait it out, but I think you're right. I'll probably go once my car is ready," I replied.

After a few tries, I found a nearby walk-in clinic that could take me right away. Not 100% sure why my cough lingered, the doctor guessed I had picked up an allergy of some kind. Rumor has it that it's not uncommon for first-time Texas visitors to have a reaction to the heavy pollen in the air that time of year. And it apparently is equally common for people to pull intercostal muscles from coughing. I'd hardly known a pain so acute, sharp, and inescapable—aside from that of the heart.

About 30 minutes later, I walked out of the clinic's adjoining pharmacy with an antibiotic prescription, a prescription for a cough suppressant, an over the counter antihistamine, and another prescription for something to mute the pain. I then swung by the local Whole Foods and picked up a bottle of non-refrigerated, plant-based probiotics. After speaking with Mom, she insisted I get them to help maintain a balance of good bacteria in my body while on the antibiotic.

"Yes, I'll have the tempeh Rueben with a side of the butter-nut squash soup, please." I said to the server at Café Samana. I had been there the day before specifically to eat as part of the road trip, but it was the only vegan-friendly restaurant nearby and I wanted to get some food in my stomach before dosing up on all those meds.

I took a few bites of the sandwich and popped the pills one by one. I knew I'd be getting drowsy soon from the combo, and was already beginning to lose focus by the end of the meal, so I drove to the closest movie theater.

"One for *Dredd*, please." I had little interest in this particular film, despite my love of science fiction and going to the movies.

"We've only got seats left for the 3D showing; is that cool?" asked the teller.

"Sure," I said.

Even though I hate having to wear those special glasses over my own glasses, and dislike watching in 3D in general, I was eager for a dark corner to relax and let the meds kick in.

I had become doubly fond of going out to the movies since being on the road alone. I found it to be my only escape from the hustle of the trip, most of the time. During the day, I was

WILL TRAVEL FOR VEGAN FOOD

in restaurants and coffee shops with dozens of strangers coming and going. I was constantly planning, writing, or driving; answering emails, coordinating to meet up with new friends, carrying on conversations with strangers, always being "on." Even at night when I'd bury myself in the pillows and blankets in the van, it was still just Gerty's thin shell that separated me from people walking by right next to her. I'd often hear their conversations and hold my breath, hoping they wouldn't guess someone was inside. But in a theater, I could hunker down in the dark room and feel comfortably alone. My brain could let go of the whirlwind—if only for a little while—and simply escape into fictional fantasy lands of superheroes, aliens, and shape shifters.

I woke just before the house lights brightened, credits rolling. I'm not sure how long I'd been out, but felt groggier than ever. As I shuffled back to the van, I felt a flash of caution. 'What if someone had been watching me?' I thought to myself. 'I better look more alert.' I picked up my pace, lifted my gaze, and added a confident, don't-mess-with-me stride, there in the desolate movie theater parking lot. 'Just in case,' I thought. The sun was beginning to set, and once inside the van, I searched Priceline for a cheap deal. I desperately craved a shower and a good night's sleep.

On my way to the hotel, I stopped by The Tropical—a hilltop Thai restaurant with a few vegan options—and picked up a to-go order of garlic rice and veggies with these huge build-your-own lettuce wraps filled with glass noodles, onions, and perfectly seasoned mixed vegetables topped with chopped peanuts. It hit the spot. I popped another probiotic, stripped, and took a long, hot shower before crawling into bed unclothed. The smell of the crisp, freshly-pressed linens softened my thoughts, and the cool sheets felt soothing against my naked body. I pulled the three extra pillows in and shimmied them close. I didn't feel like getting up to turn the lights off.

While scanning the bedside light, for a switch or knob within reach, I noticed a tiny black ant crawling across the nightstand.

It stopped and I swear it was looking at me. My eyes began to shutter close, like heavy curtains whose drawstrings were old and knotted, and only worked intermittently.

I began to drift off to the recollection of this huge piece of chocolate cake I'd picked up from Vegan Treats, months earlier, in Bethlehem, Pennsylvania. I'd had Vegan Treats dozens of times before—at veggie festivals and in New York City restaurants that carried their sweets for dessert—but I'd never been to their brick and mortar location. It felt like I was headed to a theme park. I was excited to see the wonderment that generated some of the most amazing and beautifully adorned treats in the country.

Knowing it would be a long time, if ever, before I'd get to stop in again, I stocked up on cream-filled donuts, crunchy cannolis, and rounded pieces of mini cakes, one strawberry and the other chocolate. With my treats boxed up, I pranced out of the shop holding an ice cream cone that was nearly toppling over with swirls of their chocolate soft serve and rainbow sprinkles.

"Are you Kristin, from Will Travel for Vegan food?" the gentlemen from behind the counter asked. I turned 20 shades of red when I realized it was Christian, the owner of the restaurant. "We've been expecting you!" he said.

I had just driven from Bethlehem to Scranton, specifically to dine at Eden a Vegan Café. Apparently Christian had been following my journey through the project's Facebook page, and thought I might stop in soon. This was back when I was on the East Coast/first leg of the trip, a few months earlier. It'd mark the first time a restaurant owner not only recognized me, but made it a point to await my arrival. I felt profoundly honored!

One of my favorite things about Eden a Vegan Café, aside from their scrumptious diner-style eats, was their bathroom. Its stark white walls were plastered with hundreds of stickers advocating for veganism, animal rights, sustainability, environmental awareness, and the like.

Before leaving, I snapped a pic of Christian adhering a Will Travel… sticker to the wall, among the others. Very cool.

I found a quiet side street to park on that night. As I readied myself for bed, I remembered the bag full of Vegan Treats and suddenly *needed* a bite of that chocolate cake. It was dark in the van, so I felt my way around to the box that held the captivating sweetness.

I lifted the top of the thin, square cardboard container, and then one of the sides as well. I slid the treat, on its golden scalloped tray, onto the palm of my hand, and in one feverish plunge, I mouthed a huge bite. I chewed once, twice, and then stopped.

'What is that?' I thought to myself. 'Is that? Is there something moving?' I began to feel tiny shuffles on my hand that held the cake. I was afraid to let go or to keep chewing. I frantically reached for my phone, selected the Flashlight app, and shone a light onto the cake.

Dozens of pinhole-sized black ants scattered in all directions. They had enveloped the sweet cake and were now moving down my wrist and up my arm!

In a swift reactionary swipe, I dropped the cake into the Vegan Treats bag, flung the van's side door open, and frantically shook the ants off my arm. Suddenly I realized that in all the commotion, I had swallowed that bite of cake. In disgust, I began spitting, gagging, and pawing at my face to wipe away any lingering crawlies.

I should have known better. It was warm out and the bag of tempting treats had been sitting in the van for more than six hours before I dove in. I should have checked before taking a bite, even though the van had no history of housing ants—none that I knew of, anyway.

'Okay, so, I probably ate some ants.' I shuddered at the thought. 'How very non-vegan of me. Also, ew.'

I woke up late the next morning at the hotel in Tulsa, feeling drowsy yet well rested. I rolled onto my right side and drew in the scent of the pillowcase before gently stretching onto my back fully, from fingers to toes. I still couldn't stretch comfortably all the way, but my ribs felt better and my throat didn't hurt as much. The meds were working.

It was cooler that morning and, for the first time in months, I revisited my two-pair jean collection. I had to do that thing—often seen in weight loss commercials or weird clothes shopping interactions between girlfriends—where I'd lie down and struggle to zip the pants closed. I'd gained weight. And not just a little, apparently. I took to literally jumping up and down to scooch the pants up an inch at a time. They now felt tight and uncomfortable.

I packed my things, checked out of the hotel, and walked to the van. I drew open Gerty's blinds on the back and side windows, plugged in the power inverter, set my earbuds on the dash—to have ready in case anyone called while I was driving—set out my favorite Chocolate Saviseed Vega protein bar for when I'd get hungry, and opened *How Stuff Works* in the Podcast app in preparation for the drive ahead.

CHAPTER 17

GOOD LANDS

" Captain's log, stardate 2012.335…" I began to write, for the opening of a new blog post. The last few days, I'd gotten into a routine of writing posts in a diary-style fashion, hoping that would help me stay on top of the blogging, and make this part of the country still interesting to read about despite the lack of food I'd encountered.

It wasn't always easy, the blogging. Making room for thoughts that could be expressed in evolving and interesting ways sometimes felt like a chore—especially nights when it followed long hours of driving, or deep conversations with new friends. It didn't help that a single post would take me anywhere from three to eight hours, depending on how much I enjoyed the food, who I met, and everything in between. Sometimes they seemed like little novels. Other times they were mostly just pictures of food.

It was also hard to keep my brain going. I slipped a lot, and began missing days, weeks, and eventually sometimes months between posts. It seems silly to think how stressed I let that get me—the act of not publishing new content when I thought I should be. But I made a quiet pact with myself when I started the journey: that in exchange for the generosity of those who were helping me stay mobile and complete this crazy mission, I'd give free promotion and marketing to every single eatery I stopped at. And to me, that included blog posts.

Since I had entered South Dakota and would be driving through Wyoming and Montana next—parts of the country with a total of zero vegetarian restaurants, let alone any vegan ones—it had gotten a little easier to catch up on writing. The posts morphed into semi-personal stories from each day or week prior, and I found it more enjoyable to write about the scenery, wildlife, and pretty much anything other than food.

After about 30 minutes staring at the computer and poking at the keyboard, my eyes began to sting a little. It was about 9PM and already pitch black inside the van; the hard glow of the screen burned into my pupils.

I was camped out at Sage Creek Campgrounds in the Badlands National Park of South Dakota. It's 12.5 miles west, down a gravel road, and off the main road that runs through the center of the Park. I thought for sure I wouldn't make it before sundown, and after a while, I wondered if I was even headed in the right direction at all.

I chose this, of the two campgrounds listed on the map, because I had read that it was more prone to wildlife sightings. And by the time I'd reached the grounds, I had already seen more native animals—the kind I only ever saw in National Geographic—than I could believe.

I slowly rolled up to a large brown sign, at the east entrance, with bubbly lettering that read: Entering Badlands National Park. Next to it, an oversized downturned arrowhead-shaped sign, with a mural depicting a black hills spruce tree, snowcapped mountains, and a buffalo at the bottom, read: National Park Service. This was my first time visiting a national park of any kind.

After paying the Park entry fee, I pulled up to the first over-look. I was beyond giddy. The drive up through the endless windmill-covered fields of Kansas, and the expansive contrasting mounds of dusty and deep green grasses of Nebraska—both breathtakingly contemplative and beautiful in their own right—hadn't come close to preparing me for the likes of the Badlands. The moment I opened the driver's side door, it felt as though the air shifted. It was like the world slowed down to give Bad-lands' visitors ample time to soak it all in.

Half expecting Quaid, wearing a busted space suit, to come tumbling down the side of one of the sedimentary rock for-mations, I was immediately transfixed by the orange, grey, beige, yellow, and auburn layers of cemented sand and clay. It appeared as if they were erupting from the ground—fierce battlefields of sharp peaks, deep valleys, and endless miles of flat nothingness, millions of years in the making. 'How could this be of the same world I've known and have been living in all my life?' I thought.

I followed the first wooden-planked walkway, passing signs that warned of rattlesnakes. The slats of dusty two-by-fours echoed under the footfall of my Converse shoes, and I noticed there were only three other people admiring the view just then. Perhaps late September was off-season. Though I hadn't given it a thought prior to arriving, I was glad to be able to pass through feeling like I was the only one around for miles at times.

I returned to the van and headed toward the visitor's center, stopping every few minutes to capture stills of the breathtaking foreign structures, as well as two different herds of white-bot-tomed, long-horned sheep. They didn't seem to care a lick about me and big ol' Gerty inching by, while they casually grazed along either side of the roadway. I, on the other hand, caught myself "wow-ing" out loud more than once. Sometimes, if I closed my eyes and sat quietly enough, I could hear the snaps of dry grass being plucked and chewed by the sheep, their airy breathing patterns, and occasional sneezes. I pictured their little jaws rocking side to side, and pondered their weight shifts, from one front leg to the other, then lifting a hind leg, setting it a few inches forward, leaving behind small semi-circular hooved impressions.

Running low on snacks—ill prepared for this leg of the trip— and realizing I'd be there overnight now, I was relieved to find vegetarian tacos and a black bean burger on the menu at the only food hub in the Park. They were both easily veganized with a few simple modifications. I ordered the black bean burger sans cheese and mayo, and added a side of sweet potato fries.

While studying the Park map, I overheard someone ordering their meal at a nearby table of three. The woman and two men looked like they belonged in a national park. They had big earth tone, worn packs set alongside each of their chairs. They looked fit in their hefty hiking boots and all-weather gear. Their skin was tanned and tough, though I'd put them at no more than mid-thirties.

"Would it be possible to get the nacho plate without the meat?" asked one of the men. A vegetarian among them, perhaps? A fleeting sense of camaraderie passed through me, as if we shared a secret bond, but we'd play it cool and casual among the omnis. The thought made me smile to myself. But I was jittery and fussing with the napkins, stacking tiny plastic cups of creamer, and rearranging the condiments. I had no cell signal for the first time on the trip, and it was making me restless.

I picked up the menu again and scanned it for a third time, in case I'd missed anything else that could be veganized, even though I'd already placed my order. I'd grown accustomed to glazing over words like chicken, beef, fish, cheese, and eggs. I'd become skilled at being able to quickly deconstruct something in a way that would make it veganize-able. But there was something new on this menu that caused me to pause: bison burger. 'Aren't we here, in this very Park, to revel at the wild bison? To preserve their existence?' I thought. 'How is it then that they are on the very menu of an establishment that's here to protect them?' It didn't make sense.

As I continued to meander through the Badlands via a front row seat in Gerty, I began to care less about that cell reception. I started to notice things like the sweet northern breeze across my face, the crunch of gravel below my slow steps, and catching myself speechless, close to tears, or verbalizing my astonishment or joy to absolutely no one.

"Do you see th…" I said out loud, catching myself mid-sentence while simultaneously realizing that I was reaching into the air for a man's arm. For someone who wasn't there. I don't know who the man was supposed to be, or who I expected to be there; I was so lost in the beauty of it all that I actually thought I couldn't possibly be alone for this. Not something this special.

While fleeting thoughts crept in about how nice it would have been to share being there, and seeing these things, with someone else—someone to hold when the piercing orange sun began to set, someone to set up camp with, point out prairie dogs to, and listen to the wolves howling just a few yards from where we slept—I was beginning to learn to turn inward for celebration now, instead of depending on someone else to validate the excitement or wonderment of a particular event. There's a part of me that felt profoundly grateful to be there on my own. That this was important and necessary.

It reminded me of a beautiful poem by Tanya Davis called "How to Be Alone." It went viral on YouTube in 2010, when filmmaker Andrea Dorfman created a touching visual story to accompany Tanya's words. The opening line is one of my favorites: "If you are at first lonely, be patient. If you've not been alone much, or if when you were, you weren't okay with it, then just wait. You'll find it's fine to be alone once you're embracing it."

As my brain fluttered awake, but before being fully aware, I momentarily forgot where I was. I shuffled through my old bedroom at my parents' house—no, no, my apartment in Somerville—wait, no, that guest house above the garage in Austin—oh, the van. I'm in the van. I slowly opened an eye, only then remembering that I had landed in the Badlands yesterday. Right. The campground.

I sat up and slid the sleeping bag down, reaching for my VEGAN hoodie. I slipped it on, leaving the hood up where it landed, as I crawled on my hands to the edge of the bed. I twisted around until my feet met the floor. While kneeling, I pulled my sweatpants down and grabbed the GoGirl—a mauve-colored, silicone funnel manufactured specifically for situations like these—and one of the designated pee canteens. I held the GoGirl snug to myself, placed the other end into the mouth of the canteen, and peed. I carefully set the canteen onto the floor of the van—aiming for no spillage—grabbed a baby wipe for myself and then another to wipe down the GoGirl funnel before putting it back in its container. I replaced the lid of the canteen, pulled my sweats up, toed my flip-flops on, and stepped out of the van's side door.

It was seven in the morning and I held a rigid hand to my brow, shielding my eyes from the bright rays. The air was crisp and light that day; I felt more rested than I had in quite some time, and the campground was decidedly silent.

Since it was near dark when I'd arrived the night before, I didn't get a good look at the grounds: a single oval loop— maybe a half a mile long—with scattered benches and awnings to indicate campsites. There were no fire pits, bathrooms, or electricity. It was flat, sprawling, and mostly barren. There were just a couple tents set up across the way, and Gerty looked sleek against the desert backdrop.

I grabbed the canteen of pee and walked a few feet away

before pouring it out. I baby wiped the canteen, then used some bottled disinfectant on my hands before changing from sweats to ill-fitting jeans, prepping for the day's haul.

As I turned back onto the main Badlands road, I rounded a sharp bend on an incline. I crested the hill as the sun blindingly streamed across the horizon, suddenly revealing a herd of hundreds of wild bison.

I stopped the van sharply, and the dust that had been trailing us caught up momentarily. As it settled, I noticed other little dust clouds in the distance, where the front big-eyed bison were rolling on their backs from this side to that. Some stood grazing, only 100 feet or so away. The morning shadows of the nearer ones stretched toward me, as if they were reaching for Gerty's wheels. Their thick, mahogany-colored coats dotted the orange-tinted landscape as far as the eye could see. Some were snorting in contentment while grazing, and a few calves ran around like clumsy stick figures.

I turned the van off and sat for a while. Just watching. No other vehicle passed all the while. It was just me, Gerty, and the bison.

HOW TO BE ALONE
by Tanya Davis

If you are at first lonely, be patient. If you've not been alone much, or if when you were, you weren't okay with it, then just wait. You'll find it's fine to be alone once you're embracing it.

We could start with the acceptable places, the bathroom, the coffee shop, the library. Where you can stall and read the paper, where you can get your caffeine fix and sit and

*stay there. Where you can browse the stacks and smell
the books. You're not supposed to talk much anyway so
it's safe there.*

*There's also the gym. If you're shy you could hang out
with yourself in mirrors, you could put headphones in.*

*And there's public transportation, because we all gotta
go places.*

*And there's prayer and meditation. No one will think
less if you're hanging with your breath seeking peace
and salvation.*

*Start simple. Things you may have previously based on
your avoid being alone principles.*

*The lunch counter. Where you will be surrounded by
chow-downers. Employees who only have an hour and
their spouses work across town and so they — like you —
will be alone.*

Resist the urge to hang out with your cell phone.

*When you are comfortable with eat lunch and run, take
yourself out for dinner. A restaurant with linen and sil-
verware. You're no less intriguing a person when you're
eating solo dessert to cleaning the whipped cream from
the dish with your finger. In fact, some people at full
tables will wish they were where you were.*

*Go to the movies. Where it is dark and soothing. Alone
in your seat amidst a fleeting community. And then, take
yourself out dancing to a club where no one knows you.
Stand on the outside of the floor till the lights convince*

*you more and more and the music shows you. Dance like
no one's watching...because, they're probably not. And,
if they are, assume it is with best of human intentions.
The way bodies move genuinely to beats is, after all, gorgeous and affecting. Dance until you're sweating, and
beads of perspiration remind you of life's best things,
down your back like a brook of blessings.*

*Go to the woods alone, and the trees and squirrels
will watch for you. Go to an unfamiliar city, roam the
streets, there're always statues to talk to and benches
made for sitting give strangers a shared existence if only
for a minute and these moments can be so uplifting
and the conversations you get in by sitting alone on
benches might've never happened had you not been there
by yourself.*

*Society is afraid of alone-dom, like lonely hearts are wast-
ing away in basements, like people must have problems
if, after a while, nobody is dating them. But lonely is a
freedom that breathes easy and weightless and lonely is
healing if you make it.*

*You could stand, swathed by groups and mobs or hold
hands with your partner, look both further and farther
for the endless quest for company. But no one's in your
head and by the time you translate your thoughts, some
essence of them may be lost or perhaps it is just kept.*

*Perhaps in the interest of loving oneself, perhaps all
those sappy slogans from preschool over to high school's
groaning were tokens for holding the lonely at bay.
'Cause if you're happy in your head then solitude is
blessed and alone is okay.*

*It's okay if no one believes like you. All experience is
unique, no one has the same synapses, can't think like
you, for this be relieved, keeps things interesting life's
magic things in reach.*

*And it doesn't mean you're not connected, that commu-
nity's not present, just take the perspective you get from
being one person in one head and feel the effects of it.
Take silence and respect it. If you have an art that needs
a practice, stop neglecting it. If your family doesn't get
you, or religious sect is not meant for you, don't obsess
about it.*

*You could be in an instant surrounded if you needed it.
If your heart is bleeding make the best of it,
There is heat in freezing, be a testament.**

---

*For more on poet Tanya Davis, go to tanyadavis.ca.

CHAPTER 18

MOST PEOPLE

I dipped the thin, dehydrated cracker into a corner of the white, square bowl, scooping up a dollop of creamy almond hummus. I swirled further, catching a black olive, a piece of white onion, some parsley, and a single alfalfa sprout on the way up to my mouth.

Fellow vegan foodie Kristina, her partner Bryan, and my mom were taking turns dipping into the Hummus Bite appetizer too, all of us crunching down on the rich, handheld, tabouli-filled lettuce leaf boats at Omar's Rawtopia in Salt Lake City, Utah.

Kristina had been following the Will Travel for Vegan Food project since it was still just a Kickstarter concept. We were in touch via Instagram before making plans to meet and share a meal once I'd reached SLC. My mom had flown into Missoula, Montana, three days earlier; I picked her up after a brief jaunt through the rest of South Dakota and Wyoming.

"At least we'd die together," I said jokingly, in an attempt
to cut through the wavering tension as Mom and I rolled, no
more than 10 to 15 miles per hour, over the treacherous Trail
Creek Canyon Pass Road in southern Idaho.

I thought my drive the previous week along Wyoming's soli-
tary scenic route 16A was terrifying enough. There were times
I thought Gerty was on the verge of overheating during the
six-turned-nine-hour drive. The thought of her stalling, while
having little to no cell reception, in what felt like the middle of
nowhere, by myself, was horrifying. Some sections of the road
were so narrow, sharply turned, and windy, that I thought for
sure I'd topple down into the valleys, never to be found. Add
to that the unprecedented beauty of the aqua green lakes, the
enormous mountain peaks and plateaus, and the penetrating
blue skies, flecked with perfect cotton ball clouds; it was near
impossible to keep my eyes straight ahead for too long. 'What
beauty nature yields,' I thought, all the while palms sweaty,
gripped firmly on the steering wheel.

"Just keep going. Come on, girl, you can do this," I'd say
aloud while petting a portion of the dashboard.

Tractor-trailers blew by us, and I'd later pass them with blown
out tires or smoking engines. I oddly found some comfort in
seeing the truckers on the side of the road like that. Not happy
that they were probably pissed at being stranded, but that maybe
I'd get initiated into some kind of Long Haul Club if I did end
up breaking down out there.

Before this point, I had driven through Pennington County
to visit Mount Rushmore, beckoned the Black Hills to tour
the Crazy Horse Memorial, and camped out in remote Wind
Cave National Park, South Dakota. All gloriously new to me.

I spent a night in—I'd venture to guess—the most scenic
and breathtaking Walmart parking lot in the entire country,
located in Cody, Wyoming. The following long day turned
into a night drive along one of the short routes north, through
Yellowstone National Park. Grand Loop Road in particular

appeared to be just as hazardous as scenic route 16A, if not more so in some spots.

And yet, all that seemed like child's play now, compared to this cliff hanging, heart pounding, one lane, fallen rock, dirt-road-etched-into-the-side-of-a-mountain shortcut Mom and I were on—heading south to Glow Live Food Café in Ketchum, Idaho.

We had come from Missoula that morning following a bountiful homemade pancake breakfast with Megan and Michael, a young vegan couple who had been following my journey for a while. Missoula wasn't on my radar at all until Megan reached out via Instagram, some time earlier, asking if I'd planned to stop in. Another state without any vegan establishments, I hadn't yet decided where in Montana I'd go. Missoula seamed just as good a place as any.

I got in about an hour before Mom's flight was scheduled to arrive. Going on day five without a shower, I was delighted that Megan offered me hers to use that afternoon.

We four had a light dinner that first night, at Good Food Store—a local nonprofit, organic and natural health food store—before it came time to show Mom the van-dwelling ropes.

"Okay, so I picked up a GoGirl for you, Mom," I said, removing it from its oblong container. It kind of popped out, and we both flinched.

"Uh huh," she replied, eyeing it with a single raised brow.

"The baby wipes and hand sanitizer are always over here. When you have to go, stick this end of the GoGirl into the top of one of your pee canteens. Just be sure to seal it up good and then we'll empty and clean them in the morning."

"Huh. Okay," she said, then added, "I can do this!" as we began shuffling some of my stuff around to make room for sleeping gear on the van's bed.

We camped out in a Walmart parking lot that night, and went inside the next morning to brush our teeth.

"You know," said Mom, "I think that mattress you have in there is more comfortable than my bed at home. This is going to be fun!" she said, over her toothbrush and intermittent suds of toothpaste. I smiled back and then finished brushing my teeth, while staring at myself in one of the half dozen or so bathroom mirrors that lined the wall.

"Can you imagine if this gave way underneath us?" I said.

"KRIS!" Mom replied, in a half-shaken laugh kind of way. She was in the passenger seat, holding my phone sideways, capturing footage of the head spinning depths as I drove.

"Oh my goodness!" she exclaimed, followed by a high-pitched "ahhhhh," as Gerty's tires pressed firmly into the rigid, washboard-like roadway, only inches from the dramatic drop to our right. "I don't think we're going to make it by 5PM," she said.

"Well, it does look like we've only slowed by a full minute, according to the GPS," I said, "but we'll see what happens."

We had anticipated a relatively straightforward drive to Ketchum, though we really had nothing on which to base this expectation, since neither of us had ever been near this part of the country before. After four or five hours of driving southbound, the GPS started telling us to turn around. "Recalculating. Recalculating. Recalculating," it repeated until I finally pulled off to the side of the road and used what little cell service I had to cross-reference our route with Google Maps.

"Ah, okay. It looks like there's a road up ahead that cuts through this valley. I don't know why the GPS doesn't recognize it, but we could give it a shot. Looks like it'd get us there an hour before the restaurant closes," I said.

"Sure, let's go for it," Mom replied.

I turned right onto Trail Creek Road. It was unpaved, and the first 30 miles or so totally creeped us out. We passed maybe one other truck going the opposite direction, and a few black-and-white cows that appeared to be aimlessly wandering and grazing all by their lonesome. The farther down the road we went, the more anxious I felt. Though I didn't verbalize it to Mom, because it was her first day on the road and I didn't want to freak her out.

The land was flat, empty, and straight out of *The Hills Have Eyes*. If Mom weren't with me I probably would have promptly turned around.

It had been a few hours of expansive flatlands all around and in front of us, mountains in the distance, until the road narrowed slightly, we began to go up a shallow incline, and then, with one wide arch, the road suddenly opened to a larger-than-life, dense, tree-covered valley. I held my breath for a second hoping to see Ducky, Petrie, Cera, and Littlefoot emerge from the greenery.

I stopped the van, looked over at Mom and said, "What do you think?"

"Oh, I don't know, Kris. I guess if it's the only way through. Are you sure it's the only way?" Mom said.

"I don't know," I replied, moving my right foot from brake to gas. "Let's check it out."

Fifteen miles, dozens of pullovers—for the occasional passing vehicle and photo op—and two hours later, we reached the other side. The moment we were back on "dry land," I abruptly halted the van. Without a word between us, we began to "Wooooooooo" in unison, high-fived each other, and laughed for a good 10 minutes about how it seemed as though we just cheated death. We even beat our estimated arrival time by 20 minutes to boot. It felt like a huge victory. We had survived.

Our meals at Glow Live Food Café were well worth the trouble. Rich in flavor and creative in style, we reveled in our fresh green juice and power smoothie. We split an almond hummus, cucumber, avocado, and carrot roll topped with orange-ginger sauce. Mom ordered the Southwest greens and grains bowl filled to the brim with crisp lettuce, refried beans, rice, and jicama topped with avocado, carrots, peppers, and a mild chipotle dressing. My kale salad hit the spot. The kale had been marinated in cold-pressed olive oil, sea salt, and lemon, its simplicity embellished by a creamy cashew dulse dressing and topped with tomato, avocado, and quinoa.

We sat giggling between bites, reliving the Trail Creek Road experience.*

"So, Mom. One of my friends blogged about camping at this cool place called Craters of The Moon National Park. I think it's close to here. Do you want to check it out for a place to camp tonight?" I asked, just before shoveling a generous forkful of wilted kale into my mouth.

"Sounds good to me," she replied, sipping down the last of her smoothie.

The next morning, Mom and I started the day early with a steep half-mile hike to the top of the Park's Inferno Cone. The moon was still faintly visible against the dawn's fairy blue sky. Gerty looked stunted, like a toy car — as we walked away from her just then — parked bumper first to mounds of grey-orange boulders; a couple of skinny dull green trees were poking up through them.

Since we arrived after dark the night before, we hadn't seen much of anything. Once at the summit, it became clear why this place was given the name Craters of the Moon. It was adorned with piles of loose rock, displaced boulders, lava tubes, craters of all sizes, basaltic lava, tree molds, and other volcanic features I know nothing about. I read somewhere that it's been called "the strangest 75 square miles on the North American Continent." I also read it was once used to train Apollo astronauts, for their ventures to the moon.

We headed back down the coal-colored side of Inferno Cone; spherical chunks of hardened lava and rock cascaded down

*Watch the video Mom took of a portion of our drive along Trail Creek Road, on YouTube.com/wtfveganfood.

with us, accompanying each footfall.

After climbing into the van, opening the blinds, and setting out some snacks, we were off to Salt Lake City.

"I've got to say that this is by far *the* best raw food restaurant in the entire country so far," I said between bites of hummus, settling into the meal with Mom, Kristina and Bryan, snug around our table at Omar's Rawtopia in SLC.

"Really? Wow," Kristina replied, Bryan nodded along.

"Everything really is so delicious," Mom added.

We continued to pass around bowls of creamy broccoli soup, sweet basil and Asian-inspired salads, curry platters, and wraps. It was one of the first meals I'd had in a while that was filling in a comfortable way. I wasn't tired or overly-full afterwards, but left content as my taste buds took a power nap.

The place was bustling too. Folks were waiting by the entry-way for dinner seating, and the terracotta and beige-colored walls conveyed warmth and nourishment. Friendly servers hus-tled between the kitchen and dining room, but always slowed down and were attentive to their tables.

"Oh! That's him! That's Omar," Kristina said, pointing to-ward the takeout counter at the front of the restaurant. "You should introduce yourself. He's super friendly. Tell him about your journey; I know he'd love to meet you," she said.

Mom and I said our goodbyes to Bryan and Kristina, and saw them out. We walked back to the restaurant's entryway and I set my pack on the bench, removing a window decal and some bumper stickers, while Mom stood scanning some fliers and pamphlets attached to the overhead corkboard.

I stood in line, just in front of a middle-aged woman wait-ing for takeout. I watched Omar flit about from behind the counter, to the dining room, to the kitchen, and back again. He was younger than I expected, maybe mid- to late-thirties.

Then again, it's always hard to tell with raw foodists. They all look about 10 years younger than they really are.

"What have you got there?" the woman behind me asked, pointing to the stickers.

"They're bumper stickers. They say, "Will Travel for Vegan Food." I saw Mom look over at us just then.

"Oh. Are they for something?" she asked.

"Yeah. Well, kind of. I'm waiting to talk to Omar and tell him about this trip I'm on. I've been living out of a van for the past year, traveling the country in an effort to eat at every single all-vegan restaurant in the United States," I said.

"You're kidding!" the woman replied.

"Yeah. It's quite literally changed my life," I told her. "Would you like one?" I added, extending a bumper sticker toward her.

The woman was a few inches shorter than me, thin and inquisitive. She carried a yoga mat slung over her left shoulder, and was holding a menu.

We stood in eye contact for a few more seconds. I smiled and was about to look for Omar again when the woman's expression changed. She suddenly seemed tense. I thought she was about to say something, but she instead looked down and to the right. She opened the top of a sizable black handbag and pulled out a wallet, unzipped it, and handed me a folded bill.

"Here," she said, pressing the paper money into my hand. I was confused for a second while she stared silently up at me, now holding my hand in both of hers.

"I want to donate to your journey," she said, still holding my hand. The intensity in her eyes had me locked in, but I noticed peripherally that Mom standing a little closer to the woman now. "What you are doing is so very important. I want you to be safe out there and to keep spreading the vegan message. Keep going. What you do matters so much," she said.

"Wow. I don't know what to say. Thank you. Thank you so much!" I said.

"You're welcome," said the woman. She gave my hand a

gentle squeeze before letting it go, and placed the bumper sticker I handed her into the black bag.

Without another word, the woman smiled as warmly as a soothing mug of chamomile tea. She looked ahead and walked up to the counter to place her order.

I looked down at the folded $20 bill, still in mild shock as I staggered toward Mom. When I'd reached her she was on the verge of tears. "Oh, Kris," she said. "That was incredible."

"I don't even know how to react," I said to Mom.

The woman was completely foreign to me and to my project and had heard only a snippet of my endeavors. How did she know I was even telling the truth? What compelled her to hand me that money? I couldn't get over the kindness of this complete stranger.

That moment reinforced something I'd come to learn on the journey. Something that rarely makes headlines, let alone everyday stories at all. And it is this: most people are good people.

CHAPTER 19

GOODBYE & ALOHA

"Miss, the state of these rotors suggests that your brake pads have been stripped for several weeks now," the Firestone mechanic said, pointing to a thick, round, serving plate-sized, shiny metal piece of Gerty, now detached from her frame and resting in his hand.

At some point during our middle-of-nowhere campsite hopping, north of Salt Lake City dirt road hauling, Mom and I noticed that the brakes were squeaking. Sometimes they felt aflutter and made a grinding noise too.

I shook my head quizzically, arms folded, and squinted a little. "I see," I said. Truth is, they'd started occasionally making sounds months ago, but I didn't have the courage to say so. I'd been pretty good at Gerty's upkeep so far, and was embarrassed that I hadn't attended to the brakes before now.

"We've got to get some parts delivered, and there are a few cars ahead of yours, so it'll take about four to six hours before its ready," he said. Mom and I looked at each other.

"Okay. We'll walk around and find something to do," I said.

"We'll call you at the number listed when it's ready," he replied.

It was our second day in Salt Lake City. A set of McDonald's infamous golden arches caught my eye as Mom and I stepped out of Firestone and into the late morning sun. Beyond them, in the distance, stood the massive, snow-covered Wasatch Mountain Range.

It's what I loved most about the city so far—that in every direction there was spectacular landscape that seemed misplaced among the city's towering buildings. I'd never seen anything like it before or since, and was reminded of *Under The Banner of Heaven*—an audiobook about the history and foundation of Salt Lake and Mormonism I'd listened to while driving a few weeks back.

It struck me as ironic, though, and sad—the sight of modern day fast food signage, set against some of nature's most awe-inspiring creations.

Mom and I walked to a nearby post office and mailed fifteen sets of bumper sticker orders. We returned to the cemented sidewalks and strolled up State Street before turning onto East 100 South, on our way to Nostalgia Coffee, the first result in a Yelp! search for "vegan coffee wifi" within walking distance.

I set up my mobile workstation and purchased one of their vegan pastries: a giant, sticky, gooey frosting-covered cinnamon roll. Mom got a green juice and sat across from me, reading a book.

In the span of six action-packed days prior to Gerty's date with the mechanic, Mom and I drove through 3.5 states and ate at 15 restaurants—10 of which were in Salt Lake City.

We enjoyed refreshing smoothies, colorful collard wraps, and quinoa salads from Café Supernatural. We indulged in vanilla cookie dough ice cream and frosting-glazed blueberry scones from City Cakes. We joined my friend Ben—who had since moved from Chattanooga to Salt Lake—for the all-you-can-eat vegan pizza night at Sage's Café. That evening was filled with slice after slice of flavors such as triple cheese, veggie chicken enchilada, Kalamata olive, caramelized onion, Philly chees-esteak, sausage mushroom, and breakfast pesto.

We over-indulged in chocolate peanut butter smoothies, biscuits and gravy, savory tempeh bacon, and a pancake-sand-wiched, gravy-drenched tofu scramble, enjoyed during a brunch interview with Vertical Diner owner Ian Brandt. He walked us through his origins as a vegan chef, currently operating three restaurants and a health food store in Salt Lake City.

We lunched at City Dogs—an all-vegan hotdog cart—shov-eling Daiya, cream cheese, avocado, and jalapeno-covered hotdogs into our mouths. We swooned over a spicy meatball sub and jackfruit taco salads from Buds Sandwich Shop. We cozied up to carrot cupcakes, red velvet Twinkies, and cream-filled éclairs at Cakewalk Bakery before capping off our Salt Lake food tour with simple wraps and filling salads from Frisch.

Mom had a flight booked out of Denver, Colorado in a few days, so we couldn't waste any time. Once the van was ready, we geared up for the nine-hour drive from Salt Lake to Boulder, arriving just in time for a late dinner at Native Foods, before calling it a night.

"I think this location opened just recently," I said to Mom. While we waited for the "OC Raw Chopper" and "Chicken Run Ranch Burger" to be delivered to our table, I went on to explain how the eatery had started in California before expand-ing to Colorado; the chain planned to open something like 200 locations within 5 years, an impressive and exciting goal for a full-vegan establishment.

"Wow, that's great," Mom replied, just as the sociable server set down our order.

Nodding in my direction, the server said, "Is that Upton's Naturals?" I looked down at a sketched bust of a mustached gentlemen wearing a red bowtie on my shirt. It was hardly vis-ible beneath the heavy sweater I was wearing, but the server recognized the logo right away.

"Yeah! It is!" I said excitedly.

"Nice. I love their seitan. Cool people who run it, too," said the server.

"Yes, they're super nice and make the most amazing products," I replied. He nodded in a rad surfer dude kind of way before returning to the kitchen.

The following morning, still in Boulder, Mom and I had an early breakfast at Julia's Kitchen. We both ordered a tall, orange-beige, pottery-style mug of tranquilizing chai tea, and sprouted buckwheat and millet crepes, generously drizzled with a sweet strawberry fruit sauce and sprouted almond cream.

After breakfast, we had just enough time to drive to Denver and check out Nooch—one of the country's only all-vegan grocery markets—before it was time to head to the airport.

"You know…" Mom started to say, standing close to Gerty in the drop off zone at Denver International, her eyes beginning to well. "This was really great, Kris."

Since Pop's passing only a couple months earlier, I know Mom was having a tough go of it, still working through the fact that both her parents were now gone.

"The timing was so good," she said, before pausing and then pulling me in for a hug. I could tell she was struggling to find the words to continue, but we both knew she didn't have to. I understood how much this jaunt meant to her, however brief it was. How much it meant to us as a mother and daughter, to her need to know that this whirlwind journey of mine was safe, to see how it had changed me, to meet the people I've met, and to have even the shortest of reprieves from all she'd been going through in the last year. She didn't have to verbalize any of it. I just knew.

"Are you all set? Do you know where you're going?" I asked as Mom snapped the plastic, retractable pulley up from the top of the suitcase.

"Yeah, I think I got it," she said.

We embraced once more before Mom gave her signature, quiet yet high pitched, "Yeeaaahhhh," followed by an inhibited giggle and a few clucks.

"Text me when you land!" I said, as the automatic sliding glass doors whooshed shut behind her.

I opened an eye and pressed the concave Home button on the face of my phone. 4:29AM. One minute before the alarm was set to sound. I opened the Clock app and switched the alarm off.

The Weather app told me it was 28°F at the Denver International Airport. It was the day after Mom flew home, and now I had a 6AM flight to catch. I had packed the night before and slept in the van on the third floor of one of the airport's covered parking lots. I'm pretty sure that was a super illegal move, but it beat waking up any earlier than I had to. Plus, I paid to park there. So, there's that.

Ticket printed, checked in, through security, and now at the United Airlines terminal, I sat zombified, waiting to board. I was headed to state number 42: Hawaii. The island of O'ahu, to be exact.

The air felt damp and mildly sticky when I stepped out of the jetway and into the Honolulu International Airport. It had a groovy vibe with vintage 1960s-style dark wood paneling, concrete walls, and worn wall-to-wall carpeting featuring drapery-like beige, blue, and rust-colored patterns crimped across it. I half expected the next person I saw to walk by wearing bellbottoms, a paisley print blouse, and a bouffant embellished with a colorful elastic headband.

Despite facing the distinct opposition of what I thought this illustrious destination would be upon landing, it in no way retracted from the floaty feeling of having just arrived in a place I'd only ever before *dreamed* of visiting. It already felt like a fairytale come true.

I'd be at the airport for another hour and a half waiting for my friend Chris to arrive from Boston.

I scanned the candy along one of the walls inside the terminal's minimart, knowing that the odds of finding an accidentally vegan treat were slim to none. A brown, six-ounce bag of chocolate-covered somethings caught my eye. The bag was adorned with a picture the ocean, palm leaves, and a bright pink plumeria. The bag read: "Fresh from Hawaii, Macadamia Nuts, Kona Coffee, Dark Chocolate." I couldn't help myself; I just had to know if they maybe, possibly, hopefully were vegan. I flipped the bag over and scanned the ingredients once. Then again and a third time, reading more carefully each time over. 'SCORE! No milk, no casein, no whey. These babies are vegan!'

I paid for a bag of the chocolate-covered macadamia nuts, walked to Chris' arrival gate and dug into my pack to retrieve my copy of *The $100 Startup.*

The book is written by one of the first unconventional lifestyle-designer types I'd discovered in my research for this journey: Chris Guillebeau. I thought back to the video I created for the Kickstarter campaign for the Will Travel... project. The video ended with a quote from Mr. Guillebeau, which also resides on the About page of the project website. I make it a point to read it every now and then, whenever I feel discouraged, tired, or start comparing myself to other people who seem to be making a better go of this 'create the life you love' thing. It goes like this:

"If you want it badly enough, and are willing to make some changes in your life to cause it to happen, you too can take over the world...or do anything else you really want to do. The only things you'll need to give up are assumptions, expectations, and the comfort zone that holds you back from greatness."

"Heeeey! Good to see you. How was your flight?" I asked Chris, as we went in for a hug.

Chris and I met through a mutual friend, a few weeks before the trip began. He was newly vegan at the time, and our friend thought he might be interested in the Will Travel... project. Before I knew it, we were fast friends and well-matched travel comrades.

Earlier in the year, we had logged a bunch of travel time together after spending a weekend exploring the vegan scene in parts of Maryland, which included a volunteer day at Poplar Spring Animal Sanctuary in Poolesville. We later dined out in Norfolk, Virginia, and then (sponsored by Chris) we hopped a flight to Seravezza, Italy, for their annual five-day vegan festival—after a comfortable three-day "layover" in Paris, of course. We spent our remaining days in Italy driving to and through Pisa, Genoa, and Milan before wrapping up our stay in Venice, the floating city of masks and bridges.

Chris is tall and slender, and maintains a bald crown. An engineer by day and a witty, avid movie connoisseur by night, Chris' gentle hazel eyes speak wisdom with a side of softness. I always struggle to find the right words to describe his character. I usually cave to the same ones each time: selfless, compassionate, and a kindness unlike that of anything I thought humanly possible. But it all sounds so bland and generic compared to how Chris inevitably makes people feel, and the depths he'll go to help, support, and guide his friends and family.

"It was good. Not too bad," he said.

"So," I said. "Hawaii," paired with a huge grin.

"Yes," he replied, and then added, "What do you say? Shall we go get the rental car and find some food?"

CHAPTER 20

NAI'A

The sound made me think of Darth Vader, as I adjusted my intake pattern—focused on breathing through my mouth only. Inhale—Darth. Exhale—Vader.

The ocean blipped in and out of my ears and, with each native rock of the gentle current, the surrounding sounds agitated, from muffled underwater rustling to whistling breeze, chirping birds, and the chatter of those still preparing to dip in.

No matter how many times over the past 10 days I had eagerly slipped into the Pacific waters that surrounded the Hawaiian Islands, it always took me a minute to defog my mask, position the snorkel comfortably, and allow my body to relax into a buoyed, restful belly float.

I let my arms and legs naturally drift out now. With my snorkeled breathing under control, I pushed my head just a touch further into the periwinkle water. I preferred the muted ambient shuffles of marine life to those above.

Once settled, I pulled my arms in toward my chest, as instructed. Floating quietly and unmoving, waiting.

It was our last day on O'ahu as Chris and I approached the Waianae Boat Harbor and parked alongside some disheveled work trucks in a mostly vacant dirt lot. After exchanging a concerned 'is this really the place' glance, we quietly stepped out into the tropical 9:45AM air. As the email confirmation had instructed, we entered the one-story blue building with the "Dolphin Excursions Check-in" sign on the front.

Over the years, I caught snippets here and there in online news articles of what humans were beginning to learn about the intelligence of dolphins. It was while I worked at the WSPA— whose mission includes advocating against marine animals in captivity—that I learned wild dolphins travel up to 40 miles a day to forage, play, and socialize. They are considered one of the world's smartest animals, with their own language, use of tools, and self-awareness.

There was no question then that I'd never support sea parks or swim-with-dolphin programs, which prohibit their natural behaviors and expose these majestic sentient beings to lesions and diseases from bodily contact with humans, keep them in unnaturally small and dark isolated holding tanks, and create stress that leads to a lifespan of less than a fraction of those in the wild. So, when friend and fellow vegan Jess had suggested I go on a Dolphin Excursions Hawaii tour with her sister, naturally I had a lot of questions.

It turns out that her sister is not only a marine biologist, but also one of the boat captains for the company that hosts the tours. Jess had been on at least one of the excursions herself and reinforced what I had been told (when I called the company after learning about them)—that they go out of their way to let the dolphins be. Participants don't swim "with" the dolphins, but among them. They are not held captive at any time, and guests are told to never approach, follow, or touch the dolphins under any circumstances.

After talking it over with Chris, we agreed that the excursion sounded like a noninvasive way to observe these beautiful sea-dwelling creatures.

Chris and I were the first of fourteen others who arrived for check-in. We were each fitted with a set of flippers and snorkel gear. I was grateful that we had purchased our own masks and snorkels earlier in the trip after realizing how much we enjoyed being in the water. The thought of recycled mouthpieces gives me the willies.

Two-by-two, Captain Jenna and her crew of three—a professional diver, an underwater photographer, and another marine biologist—ushered us onto the yellow-and-black inflatable utility boat with the Hawaiian word for "dolphin" printed on the side: NAI'A I. The boat had a four-by-four canopy toward the back center that sheltered the helm, and a white, coffin-sized, square wooden box sat in front of it, taking up most of the middle of the boat. It held first aid gear, life vests, and blankets.

The sun cast a gold-orange hue that trailed us as we jetted out and scoured the glassy surface for dorsal fins.

"Look! Over there," someone shouted, and we all turned at once to look in the direction of the extended arm. Sure enough, a single fin rose from the water. Then another, then 10 at a time, then just a couple.

The boat filled with audible gasps as we waited for more dorsal fins to appear while others re-submerged. They were several hundred feet away and were taking turns coming up for air, like well-rehearsed synchronized swimmers. And even though—as I had learned from the crew that day—the dolphins were actually in "sleep mode" at this time, they were well aware of our tiny boat, and started to make their way over.

"Okay, everyone, get ready to go into the water. I promise it's warmer than the air out here," one of the crewmembers said as we enthusiastically flung off sweatshirts and makeshift towel-blankets.

My lips were purple now, and I was trying not to visibly shake from the cold, but the thrill of witnessing the dolphins was such a distraction that, before I knew it, I was sitting on the edge of the boat, fumbling with my snorkel gear.

"Are you ready?" the photographer asked. "Are you ready?" he asked again. I realized I hadn't acknowledged him the first time. Out of shock and excitement, the most I could muster was a swift nod as I slid off the boat and plunked into the water.

"Stay close to one another, and do not swim toward the dolphins. Remember to relax and just float," instructed one of the crew members.

"If you see the pod of dolphins underneath you, raise your hand straight in the air so we can tell everyone where to look," said another, now bobbing in the water with us. "Try to remain as still as possible; do not approach the dolphins; if they get close to you, do not follow them or try to touch them."

I looked straight down, into the bottomless depths, and just then saw something zoom by, several yards away, directly beneath me. It was gone in a flash. Darth Vader breaths quickened, and I blinked hard a few times, hoping it would miraculously sharpen my nearsighted-ness. They appeared again, a bit closer this time: a pod of 20 or so spinner dolphins.

They were dark grey along their narrow beaks and faces, across their backs, and halfway down their sides. Their bellies were of a lighter, almost white, grey tone. 'Keep breathing, keep breathing,' I thought to myself. It was all I could do not to squeal and flail with enthusiasm.

The group of us, now all bobbing facedown in the water, watched as the sleek, silver-bodied, inquisitive pod appeared to our right and then disappeared again. They reappeared below us, and then to the left, behind, and in front. They inched closer and closer.

Occasionally a few would break away and approach one of the floating humans. I'm sure we looked ridiculous to them, but they didn't appear afraid. I saw one float up to someone's feet.

He just stayed there for a minute. And as soon as that person had even an inkling of a thought to look in his direction, the dolphin whizzed away. I liked to think they were mocking or teasing us in some way.

Aside from the rare bold dolphins, the pod stayed together and remained at a fair distance. They continued to circle on and off—even letting some of their calves drift to the outer ring of the pod, to eye us a few times—for a good 15 to 20 minutes before seeming to lose interest.

"Okay, everyone. The pod has moved on; make your way back to the boat now," called Captain Jenna. Inspired by these underwater superstars, I aligned my arms at my sides and dolphin-kicked my way back to the boat. I lifted my mask and set it atop my head, held onto the side of the boat with one hand and slipped my flippers off with the other, before climbing in using the rope ladder that hung off the back.

I plopped down next to Chris and we exchanged huge, glowing smiles. "That. Was. Amazing." I said. Chris nodded, as we wrapped into our towels.

But the day was far from over. We spent hours snorkeling in other coves and reefs filled with spiked, rounded, and brainy-looking corral of all colors and sizes; bright yellow and exotic blue fish swam by in schools; we trailed sluggish sea turtles; and spotted a sand shark. One of the divers found an orange octopus and gave an impromptu lesson on the species. We all floated in a semicircle around the instructor while the octopus rested in his open palms, some of her pointed tendrils gently wrapped around and suctioned to his arm.

Half a day passed by the time we returned to the blue building. Everyone took turns changing into dry clothes using the one bathroom around back. Bagged lunches were available too, but Chris and I had already decided we'd return to our favorite island-based vegetarian market, Down to Earth.

It felt like Christmas every time we walked into one of the Down to Earth locations. Huge all-vegetarian grocery stores do not exist on the mainland. We ordered lentil bean burgers—layered with lettuce, tomato, sprouts, ketchup, and vegan mayo—from the deli. While we waited, I skipped around the store taking pictures of all the vegan-labeled bar foods, like fruit-topped cheesecake, Hawaiian pizza, mock chicken salad, curry quinoa, and summer rolls the size of an ogre's fist.

Between the Islands of O'ahu and Maui, Chris and I dined at 10 vegan restaurants,* my favorite being Choice Health Bar in Lahaina. We purchased food from five different vegan-friendly markets, enjoyed a vegan pizza pie from Flatbread Co., and cleaned out Ono Gelato Company's coffee-colored flavors. We jumped into warm ponds and swam in the Seven Sacred Pools. We climbed slippery rocks and hid behind waterfalls, flung across ocean view zip-lines, and took impromptu surfing lessons.

We pet donkey, deer, pigs, chickens, and turtles at Leilani Farm Animal Sanctuary; and attended the Vegetarian Society of Hawaii's monthly speaker meeting. We indulged in Coconut Glen's all-vegan ice creams at mile marker 27.5 on a daylong, self-guided drive up the Road to Hana, and enjoyed a bountiful meal prepared by the head chef at the Center for Healing with Nature.

We built a sand castle that washed away before it was finished, watched surfers ride 40-foot waves, went chum-less shark cage diving, had our first taste of exotic fruits at Hale Hookipa Inn, and took a helicopter tour of Maui. We were introduced to açaí bowls by a vegan couple and kitten rescuers James and Kristina, shared lunch with Mandy and Tom—a vegan couple on their honeymoon—and got lei'd by popular vegan YouTuber Cobi Kim.

With a handful of my most sought-after 'Before I Die' items now checked off the ol' bucket list, I sat joyfully exhausted

*Restaurants listed at wtfveganfood.com/where-ive-been

on the flight back to Denver. Too sleepy to open my copy of *The Thank You Economy* resting on my lap, I instead scanned the movie selection featured on the screen of the headrest in front of me.

I knew I'd probably nod off, so I selected *Hitch*, a lighthearted film that I'd seen several years earlier. I always touted "hating rom-coms," because they falsely portray love and romance, and teach young women to covet an unattainable look or act in a way that will be most appealing to potential partners. But that didn't stop me from secretly enjoying them every now and then.

Within five minutes, one of the opening lines spoken by Will Smith's character caused me to hit pause, curl toward the window, and sob until I fell asleep. He said, "Life is not the amount of breaths you take. It's the moments that take your breath away."

part five

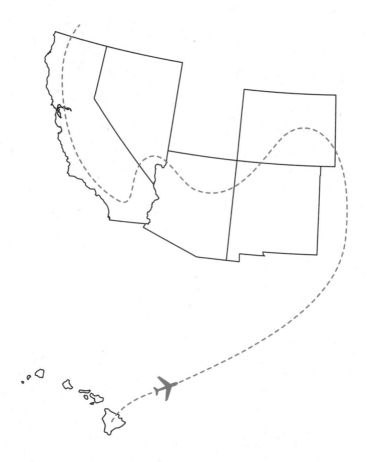

CHAPTER 21

TRUTH OR CONSEQUENCES

The Southern breakfast dish arrived. Set on a square, stark white plate that beveled inward were two tender seitan sausage patties wrapped by a heap of scrambled tofu, dressed in a mildly spicy tomato-based red sauce. I also ordered a crispy-on-the-outside, warm-and-spongy-on-the-inside buttery biscuit with a sharp blueberry jam and a cold-pressed orange juice.

It was October 18th — about one year into the trip — and I sat with a grumbling stomach at Watercourse Foods in Denver. It was my first day back on the mainland after my jaunt to Hawaii, and I officially had 10 days left to make it to Las Vegas in time for my 30th birthday.

Later that night, I met up with my new friend Heather, at Water Course's sister restaurant, City O' City. The vibrant art and colorful walls were now softened by the dinner lighting. Heather was another kind and open vegan interested in my travels. Over an exquisite meal, we talked about our childhoods, boyfriends, personal and professional goals, and everything in between.

"Do you like to dance?" I asked Heather as we tallied the bill. Her red lipsticked grin grew into a movie star-like toothy smile, and she pushed a piece of epically quaffed blond hair back behind an ear.

"As a matter of fact I *love* to dance," she said.

While Heather tapped on her phone to find a Thursday night dance hub, I went to the restroom. Hovering over the pot, I scanned the graffiti-covered stall walls. Every inch was layered with love notes, song lyrics, inspiring quotes, and angry poems. There were drawings of flowers, animals, and a cartoonish outline of a naked woman with a tail and whiskers. She was painted white, while her eyes, nose, and nipples were red. Across the stomach someone had written, "go vegan."

I washed my hands slowly, waiting for the other woman to leave, and then snuck back to the stall. I dug into my pack and withdrew a black with white lettering Will Travel for Vegan Food bumper sticker, peeled the back off in two pieces, and pressed it firmly against the bottom of the stall door.

I ate at both Water Course and City O' City another two times each before leaving Denver. I basically fell in hardcore like with the city in just three days. My time was mostly spent in coffee shops writing and catching up on email, but when I did meet up with folks for meals or hangs, I felt deeply connected to them somehow. And, although there wasn't much in the way of vegan food, what Denver did have was fantastic. The food trucks in particular swept me off my feet—Baba's Falafel and their cone-shaped falafel cups; peanut butter, strawberry jam, and granola-filled waffle sandwiches from Wafflegänger; the fruit-based soft-serve ice cream truck, Banom-a-nom; and buffalo seitan wings with ranch, celery, and carrots from The Vegan Van. Not to mention the DIY Neat Markets hosted by Nooch Vegan Market and Plants & Animals Denver, featuring vendors showcasing art, soaps, clothing, food, essential oils, and support for area animal rights organizations.

I was sincerely saddened to leave Denver when I did, but was focused on ensuring I could make it to Patagonia, Arizona, in one-and-a-half days' time for my scheduled overnight at Dr. Cousens' Tree of Life Center.

The sun began its descent as I continued driving south from Colorado, approaching the New Mexico border. It cast a soft pink-purple hue from the skyline upward, blending into a faint baby blue.

'Does that say what I think it says,' I thought, approaching a rectangular road sign at the intersection ahead. "Truth or Consequences," it read. Below it, two smaller signs—one brown and the other a forest green that matched the larger one—read, "Elephant Butte Lake State Park" and "City of Elephant Butte." I liked reading it as "elephant butt."

I stopped to take a picture.

I was headed to Mint Tulip in Albuquerque. It wouldn't be open by the time I was scheduled to arrive, but I managed to catch a Whole Foods Market in Santa Fe 15 minutes before it closed.

I used Google Maps to find the nearest Walmart, and circled the lot a few times to find my favorite go-to spot: a fair distance from the entrance, but not too far that it looked obvious. I preferred to park bumper-first towards one of those lane dividers that usually held a small tree or other shrubbery, and with a clear view of a parking lot security camera pointed at the van.

Being alone so much, and especially sleeping in a vehicle at night, I had envisioned about a million ways it could go down. My death, I mean. I somehow rationalized that if I parked bumper first to a curb with trees, then another car couldn't block me in—I could escape out the back. And if the security camera caught the action, hopefully my family would at least know what happened.

The next morning, I freshened up in the Walmart bathroom, then drove to Mint Tulip for a late breakfast. After another half-sleepless night, I was craving comfort food, so I went with a chocolate peanut butter milkshake and a grilled cheese, with a side of fruit.

They had free Wi-Fi, so I opened my computer and answered a few emails before taking a short nap back at the van, then met Karen—a gracious Will Travel… supporter—at Thai Vegan, before another due oil change for Gerty.

It was late in the day by the time I got back on the road. I had another seven hours ahead of me before reaching Patagonia. I managed about five or so before feeling too tired to continue, and was delighted to find one of my absolute favorite truck stop chains, where I stayed for the night.

Love's was a beacon of light that had come to represent a safe haven for me. Aside from that one early morning, in the middle of nowhere Wyoming, when I was thrust awake by what sounded like someone dragging the grip tape side of a skateboard along the van's exterior. It turned out to be a water sprinkler that was blasting Gerty's backside every few seconds, with its rapid-fire, 360° rotation.

Their signature cardinal-yellow sign, with a big red heart that served as the apostrophe between the e and s, meant readily-available and safe parking, easy snacks, and a shower if needed, though I never did wash up at one. Plus, they were open 24/7—there were people and vehicles in and out of the lot all hours of the night. It was clean, the staff was always friendly, and there were usually other car-dwellers overnighting as well. I preferred Love's to almost any other in-van sleeping situation. It always meant a good night's rest.

"Kristin, welcome! Here is your badge, a pamphlet with information about the center, and a schedule of activities.

You're welcome to attend any of the classes and explore the grounds," said Lara, the Tree of Life Reservation Specialist.

My parents had raved about this oasis ever since they took a seven-day stay two years earlier. They spoke of the fully raw and completely organic, healing food and juice cleanses; of the group meditations, yoga classes, and spiritual workshops; and of the people they met, who ranged from those exploring a new way of living to those suffering from heart disease, diabetes, or dying from cancer—who had exhausted Western treatment options and now sought a holistic approach.

The Casitas—a cream-colored, Spanish Colonial style building with a quaint gravel-filled courtyard—was divided into a half dozen or so two-person rooms. A peach-colored stone walkway from the Casitas parking lot led me to a steel-covered, red wooden, beam-supported awning. I passed a set of off-white classic rocking chairs and a wooden bench with the head and neck of two wild horses carved into the back of it, before reaching my room.

My room was narrow, and housed two single beds with one nightstand between them. The room spoke of solitude with cream walls that matched the outside of the building, pastel sea foam green bedding, and teacup-sized squares of European tiled flooring.

Once settled, I joined the other guests for dinner in the Café. Two 8-foot-long, side-by-side folding tables were topped with about 20 extra large salad bowls, plates, and serving dishes filled with mounds of nearly every chopped vegetable and sprout I'd ever encountered. They had pitchers of colorful, raw sprouted dressings set among them.

I stacked my plate high with greens and veggies. I thought I'd need a lot to feel full, but after finishing half of what was on my plate, I was feeling quite satisfied. It was a gloriously simple and delicious meal.

After dinner, I followed a group of four women down the Mesa Trail; they were also staying at the Casitas. At the top of the path were vast prairie grasslands and, in the distance, Mount Wrightson showed its peaks. The sandy path itself was a deep, rocky red and it became increasingly windier and steeper as we descended. Embedded rocks and square logs acted as makeshift steps in some parts.

'Focus. Stop staring. Close your eyes.' I said to myself, over and over as a small room packed with 40 or more people sat closely together on cushions in a rare guided meditation by Tree of Life founder and director, Dr. Gabriel Cousens.

I'd never really genuinely tried meditating before. Especially not like this. Not with a group of people who were breathing audibly. Some were humming or whispering chants to themselves. Every part of my body itched. I kept fidgeting, scratching, and flitting my eyes open every few minutes.

'Do I leave my palms face up and open, or touch thumb to middle finger? What's the mantra again? I wonder what that handsome waiter from Connecticut is doing right now.' My mind shuffled in and out of listening to the quiet sounds of those around me to recalling various portions of the journey so far. The hour seemed to pass slower than the third-tiered "kick" from *Inception*. I never did find a rhythm, or slip into the "gap," as they say.

The next morning, I awoke early for a 6AM beginner's yoga class in the Unity Room, located by the Oasis registration building, a short walk along Harshaw Road, past the Veganic Farm, and behind the Garden Domes.

I'd only attended about a dozen yoga classes ever in my life before that one, but for the first time ever, it clicked. I finally understood the movements and what my body was supposed to do. I even found my pranayama breath and wasn't afraid to use it there, on the purple mat.

With just a few hours left on the grounds, I managed to squeeze in a Reiki session with Michael, and a food preparation class with Taylor, before making my way up to the Chartres Labyrinth at the very top of the property.

The grey, pink, and brown pebbles flattened beneath my slow, intentional footsteps. I had been in a rush to get to Vegas— just three days left now. But being there in the labyrinth, I felt a need to steady. To *be* there.

When I reached the center of the labyrinth, I sat down on the pebbles, crossed my legs, and pressed my palms together in front of my chest. I closed my eyes, dropped my chin a little, and waited. I don't know what I was waiting for, but I waited.

I'm not sure how long I sat there before noticing I'd begun talking to myself. Not out loud, but internally. It went like this: 'Thank you for this amazing journey. Thank you for keeping me safe. Thank you for bringing beautiful people into my life. Thank you for this strong, healthy body. Thank you for an amazingly supportive family, and for Gerty, and these pants that don't fit me anymore. Thank you for these incredible experiences, and for what's to come. Thank you for this life of mine.'

CHAPTER 22

THIRTY

'I might as well be a freshman in college again,' I thought, staring at the scale in the bathroom of the Luxor Hotel in Las Vegas.

I'd gained about 20 pounds since starting the trip a little over a year earlier. I expected it though. All the processed faux meats and cheeses, ice creams, and desserts after nearly every meal, sitting to drive, sitting to write, sitting to eat. But I didn't care. It was the day before my birthday, and I had finally arrived in Vegas to celebrate the big 3-0.

I stepped into the shower and quickly soaped up. Fellow vegan and online acquaintance Paul of *Eating Vegan in Vegas* had arranged a birthday dinner at Panevino—a classy, romantic, Italian restaurant—with seven other local vegans, none of whom I'd met before.

While washing the most recent stops of Phoenix, Scottsdale, Cave Creek, Sedona, and Flagstaff off my skin and out of my hair, I couldn't understand why I felt so profoundly sad.

Yes, I thought I'd be done with the trip by then. I had planned for just one year, but that wasn't it. I *was* sad to have missed a few eateries in New Mexico that had off hours or that I didn't know about until well passed, and to have skipped seeing the Grand Canyon in order to make it to Vegas on time. But I had made it to Vegas for my birthday, just like I'd hoped. And Chris was waiting in the other room. He'd flown in as a surprise, to join my soon-to-be new Vegas vegan friends and me for dinner. So why on Earth did I feel like Sam Baker on the night of her sweet 16?

A newt-sized, plastic naked baby clung legs-first with itty-bitty arms outstretched to a fresh sprig of rosemary, sprung out from the top of the champagne glass. "Here you are, miss: one Rosemary's Baby," said the bartender.

It was the first time in months I'd applied full makeup. I had on my favorite dress—a grey-tan fitted tank that pinched high at that waist and bellowed out slightly into a multi-layered organza skirt, stopping at the knee. I had on the only pair of heels I brought with me—black velvety booties by Beyond Skin. On my left index finger sat a white, dome-shaped adorned ring with a two-toned blue flower painted on it. It had a golden Turkish crescent moon on either side, raised against its silver backing. I had purchased it from the woman who made it in Istanbul, Turkey—when I was there a few years earlier visiting Melis.

My hair was pulled half back into a subtle bouffant, and in my right hand, I held a beautiful deep brown clutch by Pansy Maiden. I hadn't felt this sophisticatedly attractive in a while. It was nice.

It was hard to believe that a group of strangers came together like this to celebrate another stranger's birthday. Table conversation quickly took off, and soon Christina, Brandon, Danielle, Gianni, Jennifer, Brian, Aurora, Paul, Chris, and myself were all abuzz sharing stories and laughs. That is, until the food arrived.

We had succulent spinach ricotta gnocchi, swirl-worthy red-sauced spaghetti, a light Caesar salad, and individual hand-painted plates of chocolate cake with a single scoop of chocolate ice cream. Crafted by dessert designer Mark, and plated by restaurant manager Vincenzo, I'd never seen a dessert so unique. Halloween- and road trip-themed, my dessert plate arrived with edible scribbles of art that included pumpkins, carrots, apples, and greens. Along the top, font-matching lettering read: "Will Travel for Vegan Food," and along the bottom, whimsical calligraphy read: "Happy Birthday, Kristin." Others had ghosts, goblins, spider webs, and fall-colored maple leaves painted onto their plates.

After dinner, Chris, Paul, and I danced to an '80s-style club edition performance by the Spazmatics at the South Point Hotel and Casino. Other guests twirled and dipped around us, decked out in their Halloween costumes.

It was a night to remember.

The next morning, on the day of my actual birthday, I awoke to a cupcake delivery from local vegan bakery A La Mode: chocolate ganache-filled and frosted, raspberry compote with vanilla frosting, and pumpkin spice with a cream cheese frosting. Also present were the most incredible cinnamon rolls and red velvet cupcakes from Sweet Tooth Bakery.

Chris had also been out that morning and returned with breakfast from Pura Vida Bistro: a huge stack of fluffy, buttery French toast topped with quarter-sized seitan sausage rounds, sliced strawberries and bananas, and drizzled with lines of chocolate. Breakfast in bed.

I scanned my email inbox while enjoying the French toast, and noticed an email from kitty celebrity Lil' Bub herself. She sent me a sweet email with a photo of herself and a kind birthday message. It turned out to be Chris' birthday gift to me. I don't know how he did it, but it was perfect.

Later, Chris and I explored the strip. I put a few dollars into a slot machine before tiring of it, then walked Chris to his car to see him off for his flight back East.

Even with Chris around for the day, and with the amazing birthday dinner, dancing, cupcakes, breakfast in bed, and exploring a new locale—one I had so been looking forward to—I still couldn't shake the depression that was setting in.

I moseyed back through the dark, smoke-tinged lobby of the Lux, past the card tables, bars, go-go dancers, and slot machines; past the front desk and lines of new visitors checking in; to the elevator and back up to my room.

Paul had not only set me up with my own hotel room and planned the birthday dinner, he'd also hooked me up with a ticket to The Beatles *Love* Cirque du Soleil show at the Mirage for later that night. I decided I'd get dressed up again and take myself out to a fancy dinner before the show. But it was several hours before then, and Vegas hadn't drawn me in as much as I thought it would. Not being into gambling or drinking much, I realized it wasn't quite my scene.

I sat, back pressed to the headboard, propped my computer up on some pillows, flipped it open, and began outlining the restaurants I'd plan to visit in my upcoming destination of California.

'One hundred. One hundred and one. One hundred and two.' My all-vegan restaurant countdown finally stopped at 134. One hundred and thirty-four. That's about the same number of all-vegan restaurants in the city of New York. And I hadn't gotten through all the restaurants in New York the first time around—I was planning to return to finish the trip there. But now I had to eat my way through the same number of eateries in California, from bottom to top.

I set the computer aside, scooted down a little, curled onto my left side, and began to cry. And then to sob. And then to sob aloud.

It was all last minute—the whole making it to Vegas in time for my birthday thing. So, I understood when none of the friends I'd invited out could make it. But I didn't realize that being alone in Sin City would cause me to feel more alone than I'd ever before felt on the trip to-date. It was a different kind of alone than the one I'd come to embrace. It felt more isolating somehow.

Suddenly I felt overweight, empty, exhausted, emotionally heavy, drained, and lost. For the first time in a long time, all I wanted was my parents. I missed their company and their words of encouragement.

From as far back as I can remember, Mom and Dad always let me fly free. Well, aside from those couple of high school boyfriends they disapproved of. But with all my relationships, work, and crazy travel desires, they never once gave me reason to doubt myself. They provided a constant unquestionable balance of soft-spoken yet solid support. They let me grow, and come to them when I had questions or needed advice. They never faltered. I could always count on their distant or close support—whatever I needed at the time.

I rolled over onto my right side, propped a pillow under my armpit, opened my email account, and sent off a note:

It's so strange... I'm really excited to turn 30... maybe mostly because this entire past year has been completely transformative for me. And I've been gifted once in a lifetime experiences, kind of all at once. The best part is I can only see more growth and opportunities ahead.

The last few days I've been looking forward to getting to Vegas because, why wouldn't I celebrate a landmark birthday, during an epic life adventure, in an epic city? The timing is just too good. Ya know?

But I must confess... I'm terribly sad to not be celebrating with you guys and Josh. I wish I thought of trying to arrange something sooner but... I guess my mind has been elsewhere. But I just wanted you guys to know that I would have LOVED to have you at the dinner and after dinner festivities in Vegas—or wherever else I would have ended up at this time of the year. Part of me is hoping deep down that you'll be there tomorrow night, in Vegas, at dinner. Josh too! It's just kind of hitting me how much I miss you all and am so grateful to have you as my family. Your support and love. It's unmatched. Truly.

I really do feel sooooo lucky to have you as my parents. Thank you for making the entire 30 years of my existence better than anyone could ever wish for in a lifetime.

Love you guys.

xo
Kris

Despite a full recovery from the pulled ribcage muscle, and the never-ending cough that led to it, my body felt done. Kaput. It had had enough. Enough sleepless nights. Enough processed foods. Enough staring at my computer for upwards of 12 hours a day, at times. Enough go, go, go.

'But I only have three states left to visit,' I thought. I consciously skipped North Dakota because there were zero vegan restaurants there and because of the mileage it would have added to the van to get to Fargo—the only noteworthy city in the state, according to a friend who is from there. And I didn't want to spend time on logistics figuring out how to get to Alaska—especially since there was no reported vegan food to be had there. So, just California, Oregon, and Washington were left before I could beeline it back to New York to wrap things up.

'I can't give up now. I'm so close,' I thought. 'Can I do this? Can I keep going?'

I opened a new draft blog post entitled, "13 Months, 45 States, 382 Restaurants & Still Goin' + A List-y Recap of The

Past Year." I wrote a few paragraphs through some soggy lenses before deleting it all and starting over. It was turning into a 'woe is me' kind of rant that wasn't fitting, and not how I wanted to portray this incredible journey. But some of the pain did sneak in as I re-wrote the piece. I got about a quarter of the way through it before getting up and forcing myself to shake it off and get ready for my solo birthday-day dinner.

Botera, probably the fanciest restaurant I've ever set foot in, is part of the Wynn hotel chain. I read somewhere that owner Steve Wynn had added vegan menus to all his restaurants a few years earlier once he'd become vegan. While the chef's tasting was quite good—particularly the fourth course, featuring Gardein—the service was surprisingly subpar for *this* level of fancy.

Perhaps I was just being overly picky and cranky though, given the pity party mood I'd walked in with.

Over the next few days, I fell in love with the lattes at Sunrise Coffee, had lunch with Paul at Pura Vida, and enjoyed a meal at Go Raw. I picked up a box of the country's absolute best donuts ever, from Ronald's, and enjoyed one of the most incredible Indian meals—and table service—at the Samosa Factory.

"Here is your bill, miss," said the server. I looked down at the pink "Guest Check" to find a drawing of two stick figures and a table. Above the drawing it read: "Your tab was picked up by...[stick figures]." With an arrow pointing to the left.

I'd been chatting with two kind gentlemen that night at the Samosa Factory, who sat at a neighboring table. They wanted to know what had brought me to Vegas, and so began the chatter about travel and dream catching. They'd also apparently paid for my meal.

I started to notice a funny thing about myself. Pre-road trip, I'd have shunned an inquiry from even a polite stranger, thinking they just wanted something from me, or were trying to pick me up. But now, I happily engaged in conversations with strangers. There was a new sense of trust and awe, though I still always followed my instinct and listened to my gut in every situation. There were certainly times I turned around or sat at a different table in a coffee shop or restaurant if I got an off vibe from someone. But the level at which I was beginning to trust myself and other people had changed drastically. It felt empowering somehow.

After that last dinner in Vegas, I set out for San Diego. I got about halfway, and then stopped to stay overnight at a Love's. I also decided to make arrangements with the couple I was planning to stay with in San Diego—to leave the van parked at their place for the month of November while I retreated to my friend Craig's place in Houston, Texas. I'd decided that I needed a sincere break from it all before tackling California and the rest of the West Coast. But no matter what, I would persist. I would keep going. I had to.

Before falling asleep that night, I opened the backend of my website and added a new quote to the About page. Another from Chris Guillebeau: "I may succeed, I may fail—but I've committed to documenting the entire process for you, win or lose."

CHAPTER 23

WHEREVER YOU MAY GO

"In a gentle way, you can shake the world."

MAHATMA GANDHI

"Smile! Okay, now look goofy!" Joe R. said while snapping pictures of me standing below the *Welcome to Oregon* sign.

We had just driven up a portion of the coast together after reuniting in Mendocino, California, at The Stanford Inn by The Sea, a vegan-run, luxury eco-resort and bed and breakfast positioned atop the Mendocino Coast hillside, overlooking the Bay.

Like most folks I had met along my journey, Joe R.—not to be confused with my ex from Boston—and I met via the interwebs. He had learned of my travels by way of Facebook and reached out, suggesting we grab a bite to eat once I'd arrived in the Bay Area.

I brought Kristan—my tattoo partner in crime from Austin, Texas—with me for dinner with Joe. She had since relocated to Berkeley for work. Dinner that first night at Flacos was a little quiet on my side of the table, leaving Kristan to do most of the talking. I found Joe rather handsome and charming, therefore turning on the awkward me, but we three hit it off, and soon spent most days together.

I'd plan many meals around Kristan's and Joe's availability. We hiked Rocky Point Trail and overlooked the rugged, wave-battered shoreline; stuffed our faces and danced nights away at the Off The Grid Mobile Food Truck Festival; and spent an evening-turned-2AM morning at a wine bar in San Francisco talking philosophy, spirituality, God, and the universe. The pair quickly became among the closest of my friends that'd I'd met while traveling.

Seven weeks, 32 cities, and a cleaned up transmission—all within California—passed after I returned from Houston to continue the trip. Those weeks encompassed some of the most unique vegan eats I've ever had, like shark fin soup, squab, and jellyfish salad. My mind was blown by Au Lac and its vowed-to-silence head chef and owner, the secret menu at Doomie's, the chicken and waffles at Flore, and the country's best sushi at Shojin. The self-assembled s'mores dessert dish from Mohawk Bend made me swoon, and the curry dish from veSTATION set my heart a twitter. Cinnaholic's cinnamon rolls had me indulging at dangerous levels, and everything about Gracias Madre made me want to sleep under the bar and start again there the next day.

I couldn't help but notice that the quality of the food seemed far superior to almost anything I'd had prior. It was uncanny and absolutely awesome.

I had a few stops to make before reaching the Inn, the first being Mineral restaurant. Approximately 140 miles inland, Murphys, California, is about one of the cutest, historic, touristy towns I've ever seen. If Salem, Massachusetts, and New Orleans, Louisiana, had a love child, this would be it. Picket fences, rustic buildings, and a small-town vibe, I nearly fell in love on the spot. And that love only deepened when I bit into one of the best burgers this side of the world. Though I'm sure most restaurant owners are proud of their meals, Maya and Steve — founders and owners of Mineral — have every reason to be.

They started me off with a bouillon of lemongrass and lime leaf with young coconut, tapioca pearls, and a black cumin and rose-smoked tofu, followed by heirloom Chioggia beets with avocado, mineral soil, and micro greens. Their show-stopping signature beet burger came topped with papaya ketchup, garlic-roasted purple cauliflower, and herb aioli on a buttery house-made bun, and a side of purple heart yam chips. And they sent me on my way with a pint-sized container of chocolate truffles that I devoured before bed that night, falling asleep in a cocoa-powdered ecstasy.

Sacramento was next. Shortly after arriving on the afternoon of Tuesday, January 15th, I hung up the phone with Casey Taft, a vegan acquaintance from Boston. He had messaged me on Facebook four days earlier: "Hi, Kristin. Can we chat briefly? I want to talk to you about a possible business opportunity."

Two months later, I signed a contract with Casey and his wife — and their soon-to-be launched publishing company — for my first-ever book deal. I was to write a memoir about this very road trip. I'd share the personal side of the journey — the one I hadn't ever shared publicly. The blog had been reserved for talk of restaurants and food. But now I'd also get to share aspects of the trip that I'd never before alluded to. I was to become a real published author!

I shared the news over dinner that night with the Sacramento Veg Society.

A few days later, I was playing with baby goats and scratching pig bellies at Animal Place in Grass Valley, and trying durian fruit for the first time at The Fix in Nevada City. And that's when I met Kayle.

"Eeeee! Oh my gosh, it's so great to meet you!" Kayle squealed as she walked into The Fix that night. We'd been emailing the last few days—she said that she'd been following the journey on Facebook and that if I needed a place to stay or a shower, her home was open to me.

"Hey! Hi! Nice to meet you," I said as we both went in for a hug.

Kayle was about my height, with thick, curly hazelnut locks that fell just above her shoulders. She wore a waist-length turquoise peacoat overtop a ruffle-y, woven, cream-colored scarf, fitted black jeans, and brown cowboy boots. Yellow hoop earrings hung from her lobes, and her left hand was adorned with a raised, heart-shaped ring.

We spent the next two hours laughing and talking over our meals at The Fix, broken periodically by brief conversations with restaurant owner Evan Strong.

"Yeah, I got hit by a driver when I was living in Hawaii a few years ago. I was on my sister's motorcycle when this woman crossed over the line into oncoming traffic and smashed into me going 65MPH," Evan said.

He lifted his left pant leg to reveal a plastic limb. "It changed my whole life," he said.

"He's actually a current World Champion Snowboarder, and training for the 2014 Olympics," Kayle added. It took me a minute to reply to what Evan just shared.

"Wow. You're incredible," I finally mustered.

Kayle went on to tell me more about how he had been a professional skateboarder before the accident. He was only 17 when it happened. And how he and his family opened The Fix to help others heal their bodies with healthy foods, like he had.

Later, I followed Kayle back to her place and she set me up in the spare room. We opened a bottle of local California White, and nestled into the couch while scarfing down a few peanut butter cups from Allison's Gourmet.

"So what's your story, Kayle?" I asked. "Tell me about yourself."

"Well, let's see," she began. "So, about five years ago, at the age of 30, I was diagnosed with breast cancer." My eyes widened. Having just come from Evan's emotional story, I wasn't expecting another so soon. I nodded.

"Yeah. I was taking care of my grandparents at the time, and it never occurred to me that I'd be the one that needed to be taken care of—at the age of 30, no less."

"Wow," I said. "That's crazy. What did you do?"

She continued, "I knew right away that I didn't want to just go down the traditional path. The idea of chemo, radiation, and mutilating my body was terrifying.

"So I did my own research, and ordered a bunch of DVDs on holistic cancer treatments, which led me to Kris Carr of *Crazy Sexy Cancer*, and her whole story."

I had seen Kris Carr give a talk at a Woodstock Farm Animal Sanctuary ThanksLiving event a few years earlier, and was very moved by her story. "She's amazing," I said to Kayle.

"I know, right? So, I started learning all about my body and how food affects it and everything. And I ended up traveling to Atlanta to a raw food school there. I learned even more about food, my body, and how I really just needed to change my attitude about the whole thing. And to tell myself that I would survive this."

I started to feel the same chills that had crept across my skin back in Illinois when Laurie shared her cancer story. There I was, having just turned 30 myself, learning of this strong, independent young woman who was faced with cancer at this very age. I could hardly wrap my head around it. If I were diagnosed tomorrow, what would *I* do?

"Kris Carr was a huge inspiration for me. I started juicing kale every single day, followed her regime, and even picked up a pair of cowgirl boots to kick my butt into high gear," Kayle said.

"I ended up doing a complimentary-style treatment, combining the fully-raw vegan health routine with allopathic treatments. I had a lumpectomy that first year too.

"Unfortunately, a year later I was re-diagnosed, so I moved forward with a unilateral mastectomy, with reconstruction. It was a total of five surgeries paired with four rounds of chemo and six weeks of radiation.

"But, I'm proud to say that I never got sick from my treatments. And I attribute that largely to eating so clean.

"I know it sounds weird," Kayle continued, "but cancer is the best thing that's ever happened to me. It's changed my perspective on life, on what's important to me, my diet, the company I keep, and even what I put *on* my skin. It's truly been the greatest gift," she said.

We stayed up until 2AM talking about family, our shared history with horses, lost loves, where our lives were headed, and how we wished to work for ourselves and learn how to earn a living doing what we loved most in life. We even drew up plans for how she could start some kind of vegan lifestyle blog and turn it into a business someday.

I was exhausted by the time I went to bed that night, but was equally jazzed to have met someone with so much passion and drive. We all say we're passionate about things. But how much is required to survive cancer? Twice.

The next day, I jetted off to The City of Ten Thousand Buddhas in Ukiah to dine at the Jyun Kang restaurant, before finally arriving at The Stanford Inn in Mendocino.

———

Joe and I traded places and I took a few photos of him now, under the *Welcome to Oregon* sign.

It was late afternoon and the air was shifting from comfortably warm, to a touch cool. I pieced together the bottom of my favorite navy blue hoodie with white drawstrings, and zipped it to my chin.

As I pivoted to head back to the van, something on a tree limb caught my eye. I dismissed it for a crumpled t-shirt and continued on.

Joe was deemed Gerty's captain while on the road with me— as all my travel buddies had been—so I could take a little break from driving. I hopped into the passenger seat and began scanning the photos for an Instagram-worthy one. 'Just two states to go!' I thought.

I looked up and saw Joe motioning for me to come back out. He was standing just off of the clearing, pointing at the tree with the crumpled shirt.

I slid out of the van, slipped my phone into a back pocket, and walked over to where he stood.

"What is it?" I asked.

He didn't say anything at first, but just raised a brow and nodded toward the tree. "Look," he said, with a second nod.

I stepped closer to the shirt on the tree limb, and found that it wasn't a shirt at all. It was a stuffed teddy bear. 'How strange,' I thought at first, before leaning in closer and realizing it had a note pinned to its collar. When I read what it said, I think my heart stopped for a minute.

The bear was about the size of a football with a quarter-inch-long, caramel-colored coat and honey-colored snout and paws. He had a velvety black nose and shiny black button eyes; and thin pieces of yarn sewn on his face to make dots for whiskers and a sweet smirk of a mouth, and on his feet to indicate toes.

I read the note a second time and then hesitated. The air felt thinner now, and I started tearing up. I looked back at Joe with wild eyes. "Do you think we should take him?" I asked.

Without hesitation he replied, "Absolutely. He was meant for *you*."

I stepped closer and gently removed the bear from the branch, carrying him to the van like a delicate child.

"His coat is hardly weathered," I said. "He must not have been here for too long."

"Joe, wait! Before we go, I want to get a picture of him with the Oregon sign in the background. To document where we found him," I said.

I placed the teddy on the dash of the van and snapped about a dozen photos until I got one that captured the right lighting, the Oregon sign, and the four-by-six note card that read: "This belonged to baby James who passed away Dec. 31st, 2012. Take it on your journey with you—wherever you may go."

part six

CHAPTER 24

START WHERE YOU ARE

A blood-red silhouette of two curvy naked women—with horns, devil tails, and stripper heels—on their knees, backs arched, and arms outstretched toward one another, were positioned in the top corners of the menu. Between them, a zombie-style font read, "Vegan Cuisine."

It was a Wednesday evening around dinnertime, and Joe R. and I sat scooched into a booth along the far wall of the Casa Diablo strip club in Portland, Oregon.

"Tough job ya got here," Joe said with a smirk and deep belly laugh. I could tell he didn't want to stare for too long at the women whirling and writhing on the center walkway and stage. Then again, neither did I. On the one hand, that's what they get paid to do: for people to stare at them while they twirl, dip, strip, and bend. On the other, there was still something about it that felt like it was rude to ogle.

It was my second time ever in a strip club. The first had been more than six years earlier. I'd accompanied my then-boyfriend and a pal of his. I wanted so badly to be the cool girlfriend who was into it just as much as the boys, but all I ended up doing was watching my boyfriend's gaze—where it landed, whom it followed—and wondering if he was getting turned on. I withdrew, shot daggers, and honed my resting bitch face until we left.

This time around was different. Not only was I there with a friend, but with someone who made me feel beautiful and respected. I also liked to believe that since starting the trip, being single, and learning more about how to love myself, I'd embodied a new sense of confidence and comfort within my own skin. Seeking approval from others, or feeling like the person "with" me at the time need only see me and no one else, had faded. It had become much easier to appreciate the beauty in those around me in a way I hadn't before.

Plus, I'd always been the girlfriend who—early on in a relationship—would point out attractive women to my guy. Back then, it was part truth, in finding someone attractive to me and possibly to my guy, too, but I realize now it was also a mechanism for attention. If my guy didn't immediately say something about how I was more attractive than the other woman—or do anything really to reiterate how he felt about me—I'd almost always feel a little down after the fact. And yet, it was my own doing. It's so sad to think about it now—the trap I'd set for both my partners and myself.

"Welcome to Diablo's, you guys. How's it going? My name is Sterling," said a young, robust topless woman with short brown hair and a pen and pad of paper in hand.

"Hey!" I said, with an 'I'm cool and dig strip clubs, and no I'm not staring at your boobs' tone.

A few minutes later, Sterling returned with an order of mac 'n' cheese, chili cheese tots, and veggie burgers.

"So what brings you guys to Diablo's?" she asked, while propping an elbow atop the cushioned dividing wall of the booth. Joe looked at me in a, 'you're up' kind of way.

"Well. I've been living out of a van and driving around the

country for over a year now, in an effort to eat at and write about every single vegan restaurant in the United States." I said, "I heard this is the world's only vegan strip club. So, I just had to check it out."

"Okay, now *that* is awesome," she replied. "Hang on, let me go get Johnny; he'd love to meet you!"

A few minutes later, I was standing with my arm around Johnny Diablo, the owner of the club, posing for a picture with one of the road trip bumper stickers. He sat with us for a few minutes and shared that he's been vegan for over 25 years and that while all the dancers there aren't vegan "yet!" all the food they serve is.

He was tall and husky with thin, shoulder length grey-brown hair and a matching goatee. He seemed like a genuinely nice guy, and had a lot to say about veganism.

"Portland is the strip club capital of the United States, *and* one of the biggest vegan hubs in the country. So why not put the two together and have the best thing ever?" Johnny said. "And, like you combining your passions for food and travel, I found a way to combine mine of veganism and ladies."

He went on, "Our nachos are among the most popular of our dishes. We make our own chips, chili, and cheese sauce. People love 'em!"

"That's great," I said. I gestured toward Joe, "We thought we'd swing by and check it out since it seems like such a unique place. So cool that your menu is totally vegan!"

"Right on," said Johnny. "I'll have Sterling bring out some other stuff for you to try too."

"Thank you so much!" I replied.

A few minutes later, our table was nearly toppling over with what seemed like one of everything from the menu. And it all tasted fantastic.

The next day, Joe R. and I swung by the Herbivore Clothing Company, along the vegan mini-mall strip on Stark Street.

We meandered for a bit and then took a few photos with co-founder Michelle, and James (that's what I decided to name the teddy bear, after the baby boy who he'd belonged to). Later, I dropped Joe off at the airport for his flight back to the Bay Area. I had a lot more to see and do in Portland—including the arrival of the parental units in just two days' time.

After driving by the dairy farm a mile or so down the road from our home for more than a decade, Dad couldn't do it anymore—though it wasn't until he had become vegan and learned about what it meant to operate such a farm that it became such a challenge.

Over time, we learned that, despite the popular dairy industry ads, dairy actually leaches calcium from bones, and contributes to cancer cell growth, acne, heart disease, obesity, and diabetes. We learned that we're the only species on the planet that not only continues consuming milk beyond the necessary age, but also from an entirely different species altogether—one that's meant to grow to be an average of 1,300 pounds no less.

We found out that, like other mammals, cows must be pregnant in order to produce milk. Therefore, from the time of their first heat, they're artificially inseminated and will be continuously pregnant for the rest of their truncated lives. And that daily milking by machines, added hormones to produce greater quantities of milk, and drugs to keep them disease-free equates to painful, pus-filled infections of the utters, and a shorter lifespan. It also means that, since the milk is intended for human consumption, their babies are taken from them. Male calves are shipped off within their first few days of life to become veal; females enter the same lifecycle their mothers endured. It's a vicious circle

We came to understand that the vast amount of resources required to raise billions of dairy cows—to "care for them" during their lifespan, however foreshortened—is, to put it mildly, egregiously wasteful. Cows and other livestock are responsible for destroying rainforests (including the Amazon), usurping crops (like soy, corn, and grains) and water that could otherwise feed millions of hungry humans, and producing ozone annihilating methane gas, causing wildlife extinction and exacerbating ocean dead zones—just to eke out a wholly unnatural product that's shown no human health benefits. Take all planes, trains, ships, and automobiles out of the sky, off the tracks, out of the water, and off the roads, and it *still* wouldn't amount to as much climate change-curbing benefit as simply eschewing animal products on a mass scale. Indeed, cows are more problematic for the planet than the entire transportation sector combined. All for a measly cheeseburger.

Eventually, after seeing the day-old veal calves tied to trees in front of the farm that lined the highway, it became a form of torture for my parents. I was in college at the time, but whenever I hear the story of Dylan, the baby cow Dad rescued, it always makes me puff out my chest a little, and give my parents a virtual pat on the back.

No longer able to pass by the baby cows, unsheltered and tied close to the base of the big oak trees in front of the dairy farm, Dad finally pulled over. I don't think he knew what the plan was, but more than that he wanted to give the little guys some company. Knowing my dad, he probably sat with each of them for a while, emotional, rubbing their little chins with their glossy pink noses stretched toward the sky.

Soon, the owner of the farm emerged from the house that was set back a few yards. I'd gone to school with one of the farmer's sons and, back when we had horses, he'd let us trail ride on his property. So, we knew the family a bit. I'm guessing it made the conversation a little easier.

"I'd like to take one of these babies," Dad said.

"Um. Why?" the farmer asked.

"Jan and I would like to raise one. We have the land from our horses and the barn is kind of empty now, so we thought we'd give it a try," said Dad.

"Well, we keep these calves. These are the females, and we'll milk 'em when they get old enough," the farmer said. "But I get $150 at auction for the calves that are back here, in these crates," he said, escorting Dad toward the back of the farm where the veal calves were kept in small bins, out of site from the roadway.

"I'll give you $150 for one right now, if that works for you," Dad said. "Can we take him today?"

"Just as soon as you pay for him, you can take him," said the farmer. Dad drove home and called Mom, who was still at work. They agreed that, despite feeling bad about giving money to the farmer, only to perpetuate his practices, saving the life of at least one of the calves was worth it.

When Mom returned home from work, she and Dad spread hay onto the bottom of our horse trailer, and drove to the farm to pick up the calf.

For the next few days, Mom and Dad hurriedly called around to all the farm animal sanctuaries they knew of, in hopes of finding one that could take him, or at least share with them how to properly care for a two-day-old, clumsy-legged black-and-white calf.

"The first thing he did when we released him into the pasture was run around wildly, kicking his heels high into the air," Mom told me over the phone. "We also had to clean his behind really well the first day. It was so caked with mud and dirt that he couldn't even make a movement," she said.

Dad was on the line too. He continued, "And the poor thing, Kris—the farmer kicked him over and over until he stood up. He was only a few days old. I couldn't believe it!"

"We've been calling him Tug," Mom said. "He curls right up in our laps when we sit with him. He's so friendly and sweet."

They were finally connected with Jenny and Doug, from a newly opened facility called Woodstock Farm Animal Sanctuary (WFAS), about an hour and a half away, near Woodstock, New York.

Tug was with Mom and Dad for about a week, before they made arrangements to bring him to Woodstock.

Nearly 10 years later, and re-named by the sanctuary staff, Dylan still resides at WFAS and remains one of their longest-standing residents and ambassadors.

As far as I'm concerned, my parents are among the most badass of them all. Compassionate, open-minded, thoughtful, raging vegans, I couldn't wait for them to arrive in what I now considered *the* number one vegan hotbed in the country: Portland, Oregon

Straight from the airport, I brought the folk-er-onies to Blossoming Lotus for a late brunch. We split a fresh-baked cinnamon roll topped with caramel cream cheese icing, chopped pecans, and spiced apples; a plate of baked biscuits, split and smothered in sawmill gravy, served with steamed kale; and a tofu scramble with sausage patties, sliced tomato, wilted spinach, and hollandaise sauce, with a side of steamed greens.

After rolling ourselves out of Blossoming Lotus, we pulled up to a quaint, red-shingled, two-story, Craftsman house on Alder Street. The Cherokee Rose Inn sat back off of and slightly above the roadway. A cement wall and staircase led to a broad front porch and large green door with a golden knob and matching slot mailbox.

The two-bedroom house is a vegan owned and operated bed and breakfast run by a kind older woman named Sandy. Every morning she prepared a fresh breakfast for her guests, and was absolutely lovely to chat with about Portland life, vegan living, and travel. Mom and Dad stayed at The Cherokee Rose Inn the entire week, and raved about Sandy's thoughtfulness and good company.

We spent our family fun time sipping at Stumptown Coffee, exploring Powell's Books, noshing on pizza from Sizzle Pie, indulging in sweets at Back to Eden, and pounding down everything from Sweetpea Bakery. We perused the Herbivore Clothing Company and Food Fight Grocer, snapped photos of our rain-soaked walk to and through Multnomah Falls, road tripped to Cannon Beach to see Haystack Rock—AKA *The Goonies* rock—and downed bowls of soy curls and steamed veggies from Homegrown Smoker and the Canteen. We scratched goat chins and rubbery horse noses at Green Acres Farm Sanctuary in Silverton, and hiked the Fur Trail at the Hoyt Arboretum.

Our absolute favorite of all the eateries was one that had us in for dinner two nights in a row.

"Kris, are you sure you don't mind going back? You have so many places left to eat here," Mom asked, as Dad looked for parking outside of Portobello Vegan Trattoria.

"No way; are you kidding, Mom? I'll take any excuse to eat here as much as possible," I said.

I had already been once before Mom and Dad got to Portland. This would make my third dinner there in two weeks.

For the first time in my vegan life, Portobello brought me back to one of my childhood favorites: manicotti—those thick side-by-side tubes of cannelloni pasta seeping with ricotta-like cheese, and drenched in a spiced red sauce, topped with strips of basil.

There's this small town diner Mom and Dad used to bring my brother and me to all the time when we were kids. It was an all-inclusive eatery. We'd go there for any old dinner, to celebrate some milestone, and to share a hearty meal with visiting family members in from out of town. It was our go-to for a number of years, and I almost always ordered the manicotti.

Together we transcended consciousness over Portobello's beet tartare appetizer. It was this saucer-sized plate of diced roasted beets with carrot aioli, herbs, and capers, atop a cashew puree with olive oil, sea salt, and toast. I've never touched anything like it since, and I thought the complexity of flavors was near impossible to top, until the server set down their three-cheese plate featuring peppercorn cashew brie, sundried tomato cashew brie, and French herb cashew cheese with a side of membrillo—a thick, sweet, apple-pear-like jelly made from the pulp of quince fruit—and two types of soft, sliced baguettes.

We also passed around their roasted corn and cashew cheese-stuffed ravioli dish, topped with basil fondue and asparagus-fava bean succotash; and their harissa chili sauce-drenched gnocchi with sugar snap peas and a parsley-mint sauce.

Just when we thought we'd died and gone to vegan heaven, the server placed two salted caramel sundaes on the center of the table. I've had a lot of vegan ice cream and varied vegan sweets in my time, both before and on the road. And nothing—I mean absolutely nothing—has come close to this decadent dessert. It sounds simple: salted caramel ice cream drizzled with hot fudge and caramel sauce, topped with coconut whipped cream and candied pine nuts. But whatever magic Portobello's staff has mastered set this piece on a near-unreachable pedestal.

The day before Mom and Dad were set to fly back to New York, I had an appointment scheduled with Scapegoat Tattoo—a vegan owned and operated tattoo shop.

Several months earlier, I'd been toying with the idea of a commemorative road trip tattoo. Once I stumbled upon Aron Dubois' Instagram account, fell in love with his work, and saw that he happened to be an artist at the vegan-run shop in Portland, we began emailing to chat about the piece, and set up a time to make it happen.

It was the very last day of January, and I laid back flat in a sweater, bathing suit bottoms, and knee-high socks as Aron etched the profile bust of a beautiful gypsy woman—emboldened with an intricate beaded head piece, black wavy locks, and a two-tiered beaded gemstone necklace—into my upper, outer left thigh.

A massive mirror hung within Aron's workstation, and from the corner of my eye, I saw Mom walk toward the back of the shop. It threw me, as I thought she and Dad had been hanging out at Sweetpea next door. A minute later, another artist walked over and asked to see the vegan "V" tattoo on my wrist. He inspected it for a moment, and then I picked up my phone to try and grab a few in-action photos of Aron working on my leg.

It couldn't have been more than 10 or 15 minutes before Mom came leaping over to Aron's station.

"Kris, oh my gosh! Kris! I did it! I just got my first tattoo! Look! Woooooo!" Mom said, while holding the sleeve up on her right arm to reveal a freshly-pressed, dark green (her favorite color) vegan "V" tattoo in the same spot as mine.

"What? Mom! Oh my goodness! You did it? You did it!" I shouted, suddenly realizing Aron had stopped working, as I'd started moving around too much in all the excitement. At the age of 57, Mom had gotten her first-ever tattoo.

"Does Dad know?" I asked.

"Yeah. I think so!" she said, with a childlike giggle.

A few hours later, with my thigh now covered and on fire, Mom and I stood outside Scapegoat with our opposing sleeves pulled up and hands back to back, as Dad took a picture of our matching tattoos.

CHAPTER 25

JAMES & THE GIANT CANYON

"Can you trace your route for us?" Jill asked enthusiastically as she unfolded a large map of the United States, which covered the entire dinner table.

I had arrived at Someday Farm Vegan Bed & Breakfast about an hour earlier. Owners Jill and Dave invited me up to their home for dinner that night—just a short walk from the guest cottage. We three sat over bowls of curry stir fry and steamed vegetables, talking for hours about their life on Whidbey Island, running the only recycling facility there, their kids, and their travels.

Their cabin-style, porch-wrapped home was beautifully adorned with endless shelves spilling over with books, large plants hung from the ceiling, and small trees sprouted from pots on the floor. Being in their company felt warm and familiar—like a more rustic version of my own family.

As I walked back to the guest cottage, using the MyLight app on my phone to guide the way, I stopped and looked up at the black sky. I turned the light off and stood there for a minute, now next to Gerty. I hadn't seen this many stars since back home when I was a kid. And finally, in the moment, it had returned—that happily alone feeling I'd come to love earlier in the trip. The one that had left me in Vegas. But now, looking up at the boundless night sky dotted with piercing lights of different sizes, I felt a level of peace and calm unlike any I'd ever known, and I felt unbelievably happy to be alone there. Now.

I contemplatively walked up the staircase that ran along the nearside of the cottage, removed my shoes at the door, and entered. The red and blue quilt-covered queen size bed sat below a three-awning window. Rounded shelving jutted out from either side of the headboard, holding colorful books and a small reading light. To the left, a narrow dark-grained table with a single skinny drawer held a petite bamboo tree, a Victorian-style stained glass lamp, and a guest comment book. Above it hung an intricately carved mirror featuring hand-painted butterflies, flowers, and bunnies, designed to look like a windowsill.

I picked up the guest book and shuffled across the smooth bamboo flooring to a large, squishy, grey sectional couch. I curled up on the chaise lounge with a fuzzy brown blanket that had been perfectly folded over the arm, and thumbed through comments from previous guests.

A medium-sized painting of a Latin dancing couple hung above the settee. Across from it sat a floor-to-ceiling, multi-shelved bookcase housing a flat screen television, dozens of Washington State information books, board games, knickknacks, and an assortment of 1950s-style kettles and colorful pottery.

A small wood burning fireplace opened toward the exposed living room area, flush to the dividing wall—bed on one side, large, fully-stocked, amber-colored counter-topped kitchen on the other. A square, flower-adorned plate held three soft, palm-sized cookies on the far cutting board table with a hand-written note that read: "gluten-free, ginger." And behind it, a baby blue rotary phone rested, plugged in.

Acutely clean, abundant in soft natural lighting, thoughtfully decorated, and plush with pillows, cushions, and bedding that cradled its guests to sleep, I couldn't imagine ever leaving this beautiful oasis. I felt safe and at home.

The next morning, I took a short walk and explored the industrial kitchen and picnic-style eating area positioned just below the room. During the previous day's tour, Jill had told me she used the grounds for kids' camps, educational programs, lectures, and that they occasionally hosted weddings as well.

I wandered over to a refurbished school bus. It was painted red on the outside, with swirls of blue, white, and gold painted near the rear. With a raised, wooden roof, stained glass windows, and bunk bedding to fit a dozen or so kids, I couldn't resist snapping a few photos of James, the teddy bear, inside.

I visited the miniature ponies and donkeys who were shy yet eager for some pets, and wandered past the outdoor vintage car collection, before returning to the cottage to pack up and head back to Seattle.

Upon re-entering the cottage, I noticed a crisp blue serving tray resting atop the cutting board table in the kitchen. On it, was an oval ceramic dish of sweet potato hash, another of steamed greens; a cup of crescent cut oranges, a banana, a small pot of porridge, a bag of tea leaves; and, in the center, three ogre-sized cinnamon rolls, with a small container of frosting on the side.

The details and quality of this homemade meal were unprecedented. I stood grinning for a long while, snapping a few pictures before taking a few bites of each dish, then packing up one of the cinnamon rolls for the road.

I watched the GPS's violet-colored guiding line and white direction arrows trace the ferry's route back over the water as I sat in the driver's seat reminiscing about the all-too-short stay at Someday Farm. What a magnificently secluded and zen-inducing locale. I'll come back someday. Accompanied

by the romance of a love deeper than a Pema Chödrön quote,'
I thought.

It took me 10 days to eat my way through Washington State.
Aside from the Seattle Freeze, I quite enjoyed meandering
my way through the rainy February streets and indulging in
some of the best food in the country, at Plum Bistro and at
Sutra. Wayward Café took care of my comfort food needs,
and Arayas soothed my curry cravings. Chaco Canyon Café's
freshly pressed juices and filling grains and greens bowls kept
my body thriving, and the folk-stomp beats from Br'er Rabbit—a
vegan band, of course—kept my toes tappin' at Lucid's Tipsy
Vegan Tuesday event. The Mexican chocolate milkshake from
Quickie Too sent my taste buds onto a higher plane, and the raw
food from Thrive rejuvenated my senses. Flying Apron Bakery
meant gluten-free indulgence and mocha latte lovings, and
Vegan Haven enabled guilt-free grocery and clothing shopping.
Seattle had a little bit of everything.

After finishing the foodie rounds in Washington and Oregon—and swinging back through the Bay Area to shoot an
impromptu music video* spoofing Macklemore and Ryan
Lewis' "Thrift Shop" anthem—I stopped to see the Grand
Canyon during my eastbound drive back to New York.

I was joined by Russ—a new friend I'd met in Portland
who happened to have completed a solo thru-hike on the
Pacific Crest Trail earlier in the year—to trek a portion of the
Grand Canyon.

It was the seventh of March, and we enjoyed a long day hike
three miles down, and then back up, along the Bright Angel
Trail. We stopped every so often to capture stills of the vast,
breathtaking peaks framed by multicolored, colossal cliffs.
I brought James along in my pack and snapped a few photos
with him and some Will Travel... bumper stickers too.

---

*Watch the music video at YouTube.com/wtfveganfood.

Hiking the Grand Canyon, let alone visiting it, had long been on my 'Before I Die' list. We started at the top of the narrow ice-covered trail, went through rocky tunnels, and on down to the much warmer, dry desert pathway before resting for water and a snack, which felt like an honor. Then again, there was something about Arizona on the whole that made me feel immensely lifted, both times I'd passed through. It was magical, really.

Russ and I returned to Flagstaff, as it was the nearest town with decent eats, and hunkered down in the old Western saloon-style Weatherford Hotel, just as snow began to fall. It was the first snow I'd seen since starting the trip, nearly a year and a half earlier.

The next morning, we trudged through the cool white powder, over to Macy's European Coffeehouse & Bakery for vegan fig walnut scones, mocha lattes, and free Wi-Fi.

"Get excited, James...we're headed to the Grand Canyon!! Wooo!!" I wrote to accompany a photo I'd taken of James on Gerty's dashboard, with the *Welcome to Arizona* sign in the background, a few days earlier.

Every inch of my body ached from the previous day's hike. It was going back up the trail that did a number on my shins and overall stamina. I sat across from Russ at one of the tables for two, opened my computer, and scanned Facebook. I noticed that a woman named Patricia had shared that photo and caption of James. Thanks to the wonders of Facebook, I was able to view what she'd written, along with the photo share.

Tears came instantly. I cupped my mouth in both hands, nearly crying out, my heart pounding audibly while reading her note:

What happened after James left us? We were devastated as a family. The unthinkable had happened. How could we cope with it? How could my daughter and her husband cope with knowing her son would never have a life, never see the ocean or a forest or a lake. Right after the funeral she packed up a bag of his toys and took a trip. She and her husband just drove as far from the sadness they could get... to where?? Grand Canyon was on the destination list, then it changed to the opposite direction. Portland. To Portland, then home. She took James' spirit with her on her first trip away from home since he was born, she knew he was with her and she packed up his stuffed animals and fastened a little note to each. Stopping and leaving them to be found and taken to even more destinations James would never see in life. They were found and James is seeing the world. Guess where his Teddy was headed today? The Grand Canyon. I guess James really wanted to go there after all.

The snow was coming down in white pillow-y blankets now. I could hardly see the taillights of the cars only inches in front of me. We had all caught up to and were trailing a snowplow now—at least a dozen of us that I could see. And each exit we passed—hours between them—were closed off or snowed out.

Finally the plow turned off US40 toward Trinidad, Colorado. I was headed back East now, and had planned to stop in Denver to visit my nephew, who had just moved there with his mom.

It was around midnight, and the Weather app on my phone read 25°F. I decided I'd get a hotel room to avoid the frigid air and get a good shower in. But Trinidad had other plans. Given that it was the only operational town for miles, in a blizzard that was quickly engulfing southern Colorado, all of the hotels within a drivable two-mile radius were completely booked. The only gas station in sight was bustling with slow-moving vehicles, snow sloshing beneath their tires.

I hadn't had anything to eat since lunch, my body was tired from driving on edge for so long—passing dozens of cars skidded off the road, tow trucks aplenty, whiteout conditions in the dark—and I had no idea what I'd eat or where I'd sleep.

I awoke the next morning in the parking lot of a Super Walmart in Trinidad, Colorado. It was quarter past 8, and 19°F.

The snow had been falling in droves and, not knowing if it was even legal for me to have parked there overnight, I got up every few hours—frozen-nosed and sleepy-eyed—to move the van to a new parking spot, in time with the plow that had been endlessly scraping up 10-foot snow banks throughout the pre-dawn hours.

Before bundling up in my winter gear that night, and then slinking into my sleeping bag, I'd gone into Walmart to pee and purchase a container of guacamole, a bag of blue corn chips, and a couple apples for dinner. Cell reception was spotty, but I managed to sneak out a few text messages to let Mom and Dad know I'd arrived somewhere for the night, while the storm passed.

My hands trembled from the frigid air as I scooped mounds of guac into my mouth.

Later in the day, I finally made it back to Denver, and stood next to my nephew as we stared up at the elevated chalkboard in Denver's City Center Park. Across the top, in white, large, block lettering it read, "BEFORE I DIE…" Below it, dozens of symmetrical blank lines, prefaced with, "Before I die I want to…" filled the board from top to bottom, corner to corner.

"You go first, Aunt Kris," Collin said. We were bundled in winter hats and coats. Patches of icy snow blotted out the grey blades of grass below the stilts that held the chalkboard in place.

I picked up a piece of white chalk and wrote, "Before I die I want to…visit all 50 states."

CHAPTER 26

THE TEXTURE OF LIFE

"An individual wants something, whatever that something is, and makes a decision to get it. Once they have it, they make a decision to take it. If they take it too often, that process of decision making gets out of control and, if it gets far out of control, it becomes an addiction…" said the narrator of the audio book.

With Colorado now in my rearview, I continued east while listening to A Million Little Pieces by James Frey.

I didn't expect it to hit me as hard as it did. The book, I mean. But I should have known better. Aside from horses, I've come to learn that one of the biggest impacts on my development was that of my brother's decade-long addiction to drugs and alcohol, and how it affected our family.

I can never seem to recall the details of the exact moment I found out he'd been arrested. But I do remember being a sophomore in college. And I do remember not being surprised.

Even though Josh is five years older than I am, we were close when we were little. Apart from daring me to repeat swear words in front of his friends and then telling on me to

Mom and Dad, to which I'd cry and say that "he made me do it," we got along well.

I'd sit on his skateboard, legs fully outstretched but still too short to reach the end, and with a rope attached he'd run up and down the gravel roadway in front of our first house, in Cohoes, pulling me in tow. He'd meet me at the bus stop and walk me home every day at our next home—we'd stop and get candy or ice cream at Bunker Hill—in Hoosick Falls, and later we'd build forts out of hay bales in the barn at our next home on River Road. We'd sit fidgeting from the itchy jabs of hay while he told stories of how our house was haunted by unfriendly ghosts.

But at some point, he began to withdraw. Not from me specifically, but from our family. None of us ever really talked about it all together. I was young anyway. But I remember walking in on some loud kitchen fights between him and Dad every now and then. I never knew what they were arguing about, but Mom would always be crying and Josh would eventually storm out.

He was around less and less, and soon moved into his own apartment with some friends, before finishing high school. I guess I was around 10 or 11 at the time.

From then on, he'd stop by the house on occasion. Usually with a friend or girlfriend. Sometimes they'd hang around, play basketball, and stay for dinner. Other times, they'd leave just as quickly as they'd arrived.

At some point, I began to feel more like an only child. And later, after his arrest, in the one and only therapy session I promised Mom I'd go to, I uncovered that my tendencies toward averting conflict, not being able to speak my mind under pressure, and harboring ill feelings toward anyone who talked about drugs—even casually and non-specifically—were likely linked to feeling like I needed to be the 'good child.' The one that wouldn't cause her parents any pain, ever, if possible. The one who would be independent, regimented, and responsible.

I see now how it also relates to men in my life in general. I had those back-to-back, 2 to 3-year-long relationships, from the time I was 16 until the age of 29. I'd find someone and hold on with all my might, despite our incompatibility. I had trouble letting things just play out or run their course. If I chose someone, we'd be together, and that was that. And, regardless if there was reason to believe they wanted to leave me or not, I was convinced they would eventually want to. The significance ran deeper than I could have possibly imagined.

He said they busted down the door to his apartment, threw his pregnant girlfriend onto her stomach, and that one of the cops placed a foot on her back to hold her down.

Our whole family was in the courtroom. Josh was wearing a fitted suit and tie, and had shaved his dreads off at the recommendation of his attorney. At some point in the last five years or so, he had become one of the "it" dealers in the state of Vermont. We lived on the border of Bennington, and he had moved there, living above a tattoo shop that he owned with a friend. But they made real money by dealing and selling—and taking—every narcotic you could think of.

One of his distributors had gotten caught, and in exchange for a lighter sentence, he walked into my brother's apartment with a wire. The cops were waiting outside. I always imagined it looked like something out of *The Departed*.

Mom and Dad had a really hard time with it all. They had suspected he'd been using, but I don't think they ever knew how involved he was with dealing and the like. And just as they'd always done, they began researching and taking the necessary steps to help as best they could.

They watched him detox, regularly went to a counselor, and scraped together every penny to find and put Josh into a suitable rehab facility so that he wouldn't have to sit in jail for potentially years. When he got out, Dad gave him a job with his construction company, so that he could get his finances in

order, though I think they secretly wanted to keep him close
to help ensure he wouldn't relapse. They helped him get back
on his feet and sever ties with his old crew, and all three vol-
unteered with a weekly support group for those in recovery.

All the while, I stayed away. Yes, I was in college and physically away, but only by a few hours. Even so, I took few steps
to join Mom, Dad, and Josh in his recovery. From the outside,
it all looked and felt like complete chaos to me.

I had become angry when I found out he started using at
the age of 13. That he had been introduced to pot and "it was
no big deal." I was angry at whoever it was that introduced it
to him. And I became angry with him when I learned that he
used to steal money and valuables from our home in order
to have enough to buy. But mostly I was angry that I didn't
understand why he started using at all, how someone could
become addicted to something, why he left home, where he
had been, and why he was now still so far away.

"If he were my kid, I'd let him rot in jail," I said one time
to Mom and Dad. "He caused you guys so much trouble and
doesn't seem at all grateful for all you're doing to help him.
No way. I would have left him in jail."

Nine years after the arrest, and nine years of sobriety later,
I felt compelled to understand. And to reconnect. It's not that
we didn't get along when we saw each other after he was out of
rehab. When I visited home on breaks from grad school—and
if he happened to be around—we'd often pick up right where
we left off. But we still never really stayed in touch between
my visits home. And we rarely, if ever, had deep or meaningful conversations about anything of significance. Nor did we
ever really know what was going on in each other's lives at any
given moment.

So, I proposed we start a podcast. I'd interview him about
his story of addiction, rehab, and life after the fact. We called it
Unabridged Addiction. We started talking on the phone every

Saturday to record our interview sessions. Through his telling of his life on drugs and sobriety, we were finally reconnecting over the very topic that had seemed to pull us apart way back when.

We also incorporated weekly video updates, where we'd talk to the camera to reflect how we felt about our most recent podcast sessions. We even got the attention of some rehab facilities that asked us to do interviews or create video pieces in support of other families in recovery.

It was nice.

We were closer, and more comfortable with each other, than I think we'd ever been. Although it has been nearly two years since our podcast sessions concluded, we still find time to connect. We don't talk or text on a regular basis, but the types of conversations we do have tend to be deeper and more sincere. Come to think of it, there is one thing he's always been consistently conscious of, and good at, despite whatever stage we were, weren't, or are connected in—and that's offering to threaten and severely hurt any guy who does me wrong. Fortunately, I've yet to employ that offer, but despite and through it all, I have always felt protected.

"Driver's license and registration, please," a middle-aged police officer said, now at my window. I had the door ajar since the electronic mechanism for the driver's side window had stopped working some time ago.

When I saw the flashing cop lights quickly approach Gerty's bumper, my heart dropped, like it does any time I think I might be getting pulled over.

"Sure!" I said, before popping open the center glove box— now overflowing with receipts from Gerty's numerous oil changes and random fix ups.

"Where are you headed, miss?" he asked.

"I actually just finished driving around the country for the past 18 months!" I said enthusiastically.

"Do you know why I pulled you over?" he said. In a flash, I glanced at the inspection sticker in the bottom corner of the windshield. I was only a few miles into New York, and had just stopped at the boarder to take another dashboard photo of James with the *Welcome to [State]* sign in the background.

"No. My GPS said I was maintaining the speed limit," I replied.

"It's your inspection, miss. It's more than a year overdue." He said.

"Ah, that's right. I wondered how that would work since I haven't been back in New York in so long, because of the road trip." I maintained awkward eye contact while trying to read his reaction, though it was near impossible to tell what he was thinking.

"And you've got a Massachusetts license but your vehicle is registered in New York," he said.

"Yes. I was living in Massachusetts before the trip, but then found and purchased the van here in New York, where my parents live."

He shot a pensive glance and then said, "I totally get it. I have a daughter about your age and she took a road trip last summer in an old van. Her Mom and I were nervous about it, but I think it was really good for her," he said while pulling out a pen and pad.

He started scribbling something on the pad of paper, and I began to sweat. With a stern look he said, "Your tailpipe is too loud. I'm giving you a temporary pass to get it checked out and fixed. This is not a ticket, but it does expire in one week. Do you understand what I'm saying?" he asked.

"Oh yes, thank you so much!" I replied.

"I'm glad you had a safe trip. Now be careful making your way back home," he said, and then turned and walked away.

Three hours later, I was in Syracuse, ordering a chicken salad sandwich and a rich chocolate peanut butter "Earth Crisis" milkshake from Strong Hearts Café. I was joined by Chris and Jon, the dashing duo behind popular YouTube show, *The Vegan Zombie*.

Just two and a half hours until I would be home.

CHAPTER 27

WITH EVERY FIBER

"Because in the end the only way that we can measure the significance of our own lives, is by valuing the lives of others"

THE LIFE OF DAVID GAYLE

On August 11, 2013 I walked out of Tiny Empire on North 6th Street in Brooklyn holding a pineapple, banana, ginger, mint, and hemp milk smoothie, and a raw kale salad. At vegan eatery number 547, I had finally, on that day, in that moment, completed the mission I'd set out to achieve two years earlier. Forty-eight states, and more than 39,000 van-dwelling miles later, I had officially dined at every single all-vegan establishment in the United States.

Wow.

What does one do with oneself when they've reached a goal that had seemed near impossible, unattainable even, for so long? They eat, of course.

I sat on the wooden bench—with a small kale patch growing in the planter beside it—in front of number 547, sipping the sweet smoothie as I watched hipsters huddle under awnings for shade, and weekend shoppers stroll slowly, one arm draped with at least four bags and a cup of coffee held in the other hand.

I sold Gerty shortly after returning to New York, back in March, five months ago. It was sad, but seemed like the right thing to do. Our time together had ended. She'd been good to me. And I couldn't just leave her to rot away once I moved to NYC for the summer. She went to a good home, though, to a vegan couple from Detroit. They send me pictures of her every now and then, off on her new adventures.

Sometimes I think back to the elderly couple that sold me the van. They were shocked when I told them what my plans for her were. I don't think they believed she'd make it. And to the mechanic who gave her a tune-up before I embarked on this journey. He told Dad it was a bad idea. That she wouldn't last more than a few months. But we did make it. Together. In one piece.

There's one literal image of us—Gerty and me—returning home that's burned into my memory, I suspect it always will be engrained, because of what happened a few days after it was taken.

I had snapped the photo a moment after we pulled into my parents' driveway. It's of Gerty's nose a few feet from the fencing in our backyard, and on the other side, Spirit, the very first equine to set foot on our property. She had been in our family for more than 20 years, and was now the last of our horses.

Her coat was still thick and fuzzy from the fading winter chill. Her stout neck was firm against the top railing, and her ears perked sharply, straight at me. She always loved to see and hear trucks, trailers, and big vehicles pull into the driveway. When they did, she'd trot up to the fence and whinny a few times, seeking a return call from the possibility of another horse.

She had to lift her head to get it over the top railing, but could then stand comfortably looking over. On this day, though, she seemed so eager and happy to see Gerty that I thought she could have pressed into and broken through the fence had she been any younger than 30.

Having grown up with horses is something I've gotten flack for from some in the vegan community. More so, that I used to ride them for pleasure, show them in competitions for ribbons and trophies, and even had planned to make a living from training them to move in ways that were perhaps unnatural to their born gaits and rhythms.

It's something I still struggle with. A lot. Not that horses were in my life, but that I fear they never will be again, because of my view now on animal rights. Despite this view, I would never take away or change the 16 years I spent working with horses. The depths to which that time in my life shaped me, and led me to this time, are profoundly beautiful and clear. Trying to put words to how deeply connected I feel to horses seems impossible. To explain the lessons of responsibility, hard work, and softness I learned from them is difficult, and it's even tougher to articulate how a creature so big and strong taught me empathy, compassion, and the power of subtle body language.

It was never about doing something for the sake of doing it, or winning prizes, or eventually being compensated to help others with their horses; it was about an overwhelming spiritual connection to a nonhuman animal that I've yet to feel with any other being or life experience. It had become about the mystery that was a give-and-take, a mutual understanding of respect, and the desire to be in each other's company. After some time with some horses—and Spirit in particular—it was almost as if we could read each other's minds. I'd stand next to her, no halter or lead rope, look to the left, think "left," and together we'd start walking left—at the same exact time. Our legs in unison. It was practically magical.

"Kris, wake up! Come quick—I can't get Spirit to stand up," Mom said, standing at the bedroom door, now flung open. Startled, Fenny cat leapt up and scurried under the bed.

"What? Oh. Okay," I said, still waking up to the thought and processing what Mom had just said.

I noticed that Spirit had been acting out of character when I returned home. The window view from our kitchen table overlooked the pastures, and there was an evening when Spirit was lying flat on her side. This would have been normal for her if it were an early sunny morning bask. But it was early evening then, and she didn't respond or lift an ear when Dad had whistled to get her attention. I went out that night and, as I approached, she stood up quickly, as though I'd startled her, which was also unusual. If she had been comfortable and sunbathing, she would have let me sit by her side, like she'd done dozens of times before. Something wasn't right.

In the garage, I threw on a pair of muck boots and a winter jacket, and rushed to the paddock. Mom was knelt down by Spirit's head, and Dad was walking to the barn to retrieve a lead rope.

"She won't stand up, Kris. She won't get up," Mom said, now through cracked words and streaming tears. That achy back-of-throat feeling crept in as I approached the paddock, and panic began to touch my heart and seep into my breath.

"Spir!" I shouted, "Spir, get up!" I said, walking up to her. Mom stood and I knelt in her place. Spirit looked up at me with big liquid-brown eyes, now tired and bloodshot in the corners. She wasn't okay.

"I'm going to go call the vet," Mom said. "You and Dad try to get her up and walking."

When a horse lies flat on their side and refuses to stand with a little encouragement, it is indicative of a serious problem. There are many reasons for an unhealthy downed horse, but— given Spirit's age and what little appetite she had that week—it was likely she was colicking, which can mean an obstruction, inflammation, or ulceration of the gastrointestinal tract.

It's recommended that the horse be walked continuously to help move potential obstructions along, like when pregnant women are encouraged to walk around to induce labor. It can be uncomfortable, but necessary.

We heaved and hollered until she was sitting up, like a dog would on their belly, legs splayed frontward. And finally, after a few more tugs, she was back on her feet and, by the time the vet arrived, she was letting us walk alongside her. But her stride seemed short and strained, as if she stepped with a hiccup on one side.

The day seemed endless, but the hours went fast as the vet and my parents let me make the final decision.

She was standing, still and sedated now. Her breath abated, and the rectal exam and stomach tube both determined that her intestines were obstructed to a degree that would require surgery. But she was too old for surgery. Even if we attempted it, would it be worth putting her through that?

"But how is this right, that we get to decide her fate?" I said through sobs and heaving breaths. "It's not right. What if she isn't as sick as we think she is? What if she'll be better tomorrow? What if it's not her time and we make a mistake?"

I sat on an overturned bucket, Dad holding Spirit steady by the lead, and Mom rubbing my back. The vet had walked back to his truck—just on the other side of the fence—waiting for me to give the final yes. Or no.

"Dad and I think it's the humane thing to do, Kris," Mom said. "She's in pain and she probably wouldn't make it through a surgery. But it is your decision."

The vet was kind and gentle. He had spent the better part of the day with us giving feedback, being supportive, and patiently waiting for me to make a decision. I could tell he agreed it was time to say goodbye.

I knew they were right, but it didn't make verbalizing it any easier. We slowly walked her to a part of the far paddock where Amber—Mom's favorite Morgan mare—had been put to rest a few years earlier. I was in the lead, and Mom and Dad were flanked on either side of her. The vet followed with a syringe the size of my forearm.

Dad, Mom, and I now huddled together. I stood at Spirit's nose, holding a kiss to it. Dad scratched her forelock, and Mom held an open palm to Spir's neck. We stood that way for a long while.

"Are you ready?" asked the vet. I could tell all their eyes were on me. I nodded.

"I love you, Spir," I said quietly. "I love you so much."

"Please be careful, and don't be alarmed," the vet said. "Sometimes they go down quickly, but she won't be in pain."

I stopped breathing from shock at the sight of her body, stiffening and perching. Her knees locked and her eyes widened—I'd only seen that before when she was completely panicked. Just as quickly as they'd bellowed open, they softened, her knees buckled, and in a single motion, she fell hard to the ground.

"Are you okay?" the vet asked, looking at Dad. Spir had landed on his leg, but he'd already gotten out from under her.

"Yes, I'm okay," Dad said.

The vet had followed her to the ground, the needle still in her vein. Mom swept a hand under her right eye to close it, so it wouldn't rest open on the dirt. "She's almost gone," the vet said, now with a stethoscope pressed against her side.

"Love you, Spir," Mom whispered, touching fingers to lips, and then to Spirit's nose.

"Love you, pone" Dad said.

"She's passed," said the vet.

Mom covered Spirit in her winter blanket, and Dad escorted the vet back to his truck.

"I think I'll stay here a while," I said to Mom.

"Okay. I'll be inside if you need me," she said.

I sat on the ground, folded over in disbelief, tucked beneath the arch of Spir's neck. I ran a trembling hand over her velvet muzzle. It had become speckled with grey hair among the light and dark browns. For the first time, her perfect nose was cool and lifeless. Its subtle muscularity was gone. It no longer blew out warm breath or sniffed around my palm seeking treats.

Our bodies were both still there, both 30 years old. We grew up together. We played, and taught, and lounged together. And now she was gone. It felt like the end of an era. A segment of my life now over. A life that defined me for so long, a reflection of my childhood that left me feeling connected—with every fiber of my soul—to another sentient being on a level that could never be matched.

I was her champion, and she mine.

"I'm so sorry, Kris." I looked up and saw Josh kneeling a few feet away. I'm not sure how long I'd been sitting with her. I hadn't even heard him approach. "Do you want to go in for some food?" he asked.

"Yeah, that would be good." I said. I stood up and realized I was still wearing borrowed pajamas from Mom, Dad's muck boots, and my winter coat. Josh hugged me. We walked in silence back to the house.

———

While living in NYC for the summer to finish my trip, I created a morning routine for myself to help get each day started in such a way that maximized my productivity. It involved meditating, journaling, drinking lemon water, creating a non-negotiable schedule for myself, and revisiting my financial life plan.

The full duration of the journey, and then some, was funded by every last bit of my own savings, some shiny new credit cards, and, *more significantly*, by the kindness of thousands of generous individuals. Transitioning from living completely off savings and donations back to earning an income again proved a slow and arduous passage, but I was motivated and excited to continue shaping this life I had only begun learning how to create.

It was during this time—particularly when I'd meditate—that I realized the closing of the trip itself no longer felt like the beginning of the end, but more like the beginning of a beginning. Of a life I'd designed for myself around the things that brought me the most joy. It was really happening!

Going back to a traditional desk job was out of the question. No, living out of a van and traveling full-time was no longer a goal or a short-term bucket-list dream—it was simply the way I had lived for two years. It was my lifestyle. One that I happened to share through Facebook, Instagram, YouTube, Twitter, email, and a project-specific website.

And now that it's done, I'm committed to shaping my passions into a profitable, sustainable, and scalable career so that I can continue to travel, work remotely for myself—wherever there is internet will do—pick up and go whenever the timing feels right, stay, fall in love, hunker down, be spontaneous, or not. Like my friend Kelly Holt once said, "It's not seeing what's out there and how to fit in, but how to create a life that fits [me]."

When I started this journey, I was simply heeding a call that I couldn't ignore. A deep desire for something different. For change. Whatever that meant.

I had no idea that documenting the journey through a blog and social media would lead to hearing from dozens of people who were inspired to start living vegan, or were excited to learn about how easy it is to travel while maintaining a vegan lifestyle. It also became a tool for deepening my own love and commitment to veganism. And I never dreamed it would lead to new career opportunities, and the development of new skill sets to boot.

One afternoon, a few months after the trip had formally come to an end, I randomly picked up an old journal I kept before this adventure began. It was the one I used to take notes in while reading Tim Ferriss, Gary Vaynerchuk, Chris Guillebeau, and the like.

I hadn't opened the journal in over a year, and now, as I thumbed through its worn, scribbled pages, I stopped at a list of 10 numbered life goals, dated April 2011. Number one read, "Visit every state/spend one year traveling the country." And number seven: "Get published."

Amazing.

James the teddy bear has gone on to new adventures as well. My dear friend Annie had come to New York to visit during the end-of-road-trip party in Manhattan that summer. She sat me down and shared a retelling of a dream she'd had, wherein a pair of hands had reached toward her, holding James, and she heard a voice say, "Don't forget the bear."

It sounds silly, but we were both in tears at the understanding that it was she who would next take James, wherever she might go. We even started a "Will Travel for Baby James" Facebook page to track his ongoing adventures with future travelers.

After New York City, I moved to Chicago to trade free housing for free marketing consulting with a seitan production company. Once our contract ended, I didn't feel ready to leave a city I'd long loved, so I rented a place for a few more months, before finally making it up to Fargo, North Dakota—state number 49. I stayed with a vegan friend there for about seven weeks before spending two weeks of June in Seattle, the first week of July in Alaska (state number 50), and then plotted a course for Hawaii. I'd been feeling that "tropical" was the right setting to finish book writing, slow down a bit, regroup from the ongoing travels, and focus on taking better care of myself, physically and spiritually. So, here I am, writing these words to you now, from a bungalow on stilts, with an ocean view, on the Big Island.

This journey taught me many things, including clueing me in to an interesting trend—that restaurants with fewer menu options typically serve better food overall. More importantly, though, I learned that I want to be good *with* someone, not *for* someone; that it's okay to love myself first; that being emotionally healthy is just as important as being physically healthy; that stuffed animals can connect strangers; that love doesn't lose meaning if it's one-sided; that manifestation is real if you believe in it; that one person or a singular project *can* change the lives of many (both human and nonhuman); and that, if you want something badly enough, you'll find a way to make it happen.

For my heart and soul, for love of self, for the lessons, *and* for vegan food everywhere—I will travel.

May we all give ourselves permission to be led by our passions and intuition.

ACKNOWLEDGEMENTS

This journey would not have been possible without the unending support of a one Christopher Zahka. Your kindness, openness, and unyielding passion for going WAY above and beyond to help others is of a degree I didn't know was humanly possible. Thank you for believing in this project and for helping me make (more than one of) my dreams come true.

I can only imagine how difficult it could be to reveal to one's parents and family a decision to quit your job and live out of a vehicle in order to eat food and travel indefinitely while living off donations. The reason I can only *imagine* this is because I had absolutely no hesitation in sharing these exact intentions with my family. I knew they'd be behind me 100%, as they've always been. Josh, thank you for demonstrating persistence, inner-strength, and the resolve to push forward, no matter the circumstances. Dad, thank you for encouraging me to know that I can be, do, and have whatever my heart desires; for teaching me to be an independent, strong, and confident woman, and to always look up and into my corners. Mom, thank you for being a true example of someone who is nonjudgmental and deeply compassionate, for treating me like an equal, for being my best friend, and for exemplifying the epitome of the type of person I wish to be someday. Josh, Dad, and Mom, thank you for your strength, your trust, and your unending support. No matter what crazy ideas I come up with, I know you will be beside me every step of the way. I love you guys!

Thank you to Ryan Delano, who tipped me over the spiritual edge and spent countless hours constructing insightful and educational feedback for me throughout a very crucial and emotional portion of the journey.

To Ethan Dussault, thank you for your myriad contributions to the preparation and early stages of the Will Travel… project. I am forever grateful to you for your generosity, your commitment, and your time.

If it weren't for Aurelia D'Andrea I don't know that I would have completed this book at all. She kindly agreed to be my accountability partner throughout the entire book writing process—meeting with me weekly to check-in, give critical feedback on draft chapters and, most importantly, providing the emotional support to keep me pushing forward. Aurelia, thank you for your generosity and patience.

To my primary editor, Dianne Purdie, thank you for being the kindest sounding board and book-writing mother hen a gal could ask for. Your uplifting and constructive feedback is largely what has made this book something I am extremely proud to share.

Zoë Eisenberg reached out to me early on in my road trip. She let me sleep on her couch in Connecticut, and we remained internet acquaintances afterwards. As the road trip came to a close, I learned that she had moved to Hawaii. Yearning for a tropical escape from the hectic-ness of my travels, Zoë took the lead on finding me housing in her neighborhood on the Big Island. As I write these words, I'm sitting in a beautiful raised bungalow with an ocean view and a backyard that meets Zoë's backyard. Zoë, thank you for taking the time to help get me to Hawaii, for being the catalyst of RAWgust, daily smoothies, stick-shift driving, and Hawaiian adventures. Thank you for providing crucial editorial feedback on the book as well.

To Miguel Danielson and the city of Fargo, North Dakota, thank you for taking me in, feeding me, introducing me to game-changers, explorers, and the local vegan scene. You were with me during the most difficult part of the book writing process: the first few chapters.

Few people would open their home to a complete stranger for weeks on end, invite them to spend holidays with their family, and integrate them into their social circles without question. Craig Wilkins played a significant role in the Texas portion of my travels, and beyond. I wish that I had the space here to share more about our time together. Alas, the beautiful story of Craig, his family, and his bestie, Amanda Martinez, did not make it into the book. Craig, please know that our time together, and your friendship, meant the world. Thank you for being you.

The odds of running into someone in three different locations around the country within the span of one year is highly unlikely given both parties were constantly on the move. Kristan Robinson, thank you for reaching out, staying in touch, convincing me to get matching tattoos with you, and keeping me afloat throughout the last leg of my journey in New York City.

Joe Rakowski, thank you for opening your heart, your arms, and your adventurous side to me. I am forever grateful for the introduction to Baby James, and for your laborious and emotional support during the end-of-trip party. Your presence during my first big exhale at the realization the journey had come to an end is more important than I could possibly express.

James Bowdry and family, thank you for choosing me to be a part of your incredible journey. You've changed the lives of many, including mine.

Thank you to Joseph Pierandozzi for loving me through a huge life change, and supporting me even as our lives moved apart from one another. Thank you for staying in touch and helping me through portions of the book writing process. I am so grateful that you came into my life.

Claire Blechman, thank you for volunteering practical assistance through a nerve-wracking portion of this overall process. Your generosity is much appreciated.

Thank you to the core group of strong, smart, and ever-supportive female entrepreneurs who were the first to hear about the idea of this project, and the first to tell me I should absolutely do it: Karen Scalia, Corey Grant, Annie Hall, Maggie Hall, Jennifer Campbell, Ace Peckham, Kate Cotter, Kelly Holt, Heidi Cavanaugh, Melanie Lary, Alyssa Lary, and the rest of the amazing Impractical Pantry crew.

To Vegan Publishers, Casey and Christen, thank you for reaching out, believing in me, and working through newbie-writer-fun-times. I am eternally grateful for the opportunity. You are the reason I am officially a real-life published author.

Thank you to those of you who believed in the project from day one by donating to the Kickstarter campaign: Christopher Zahka, Stage Presence, Johana Presence, Eli Wylen, Stanley Cruden, Karol Gajda, Pete Mellor, VegDining.com, Jeff Schwotzer, Dave Lajeunesse, Jan Lajeunesse, Annie H., Joseph Pierandozzi, Kim Provensal, Samuel Hartman, Jill Pyle, Michael Aquino, Meredith Simonds, Eric Damon Walters, Nikki Hill, Ashley Kiefer, Rob Hamilton, Terri Coles, Elise Desaulniers, Heidi, Meghan, Meredith Snyder, Liz Dee, Valerie Goodman, Jonathan Hughes, Josh Hailey, Lisa Kalner Williams, Susan Peterson, Karen Mallonee, Kelly Bennett, Russell Elleven, Stanley Cruden, Rick Jacobson, Stephanie Williams-Johnson, Mary Beth King, Dennis Pamlin, Nichelle Nicholes, Lisa G., Katherine E. Cunningham, Max Spiker, Varun, Kristina Genova-Nilson, Seth Freytag, Mirek M., Roberta Schiff, Pamela Turick, Lynn Harmet, Scytrin dai Kinthra, Elana Pessin, Bob Brunsden, Tabitha Bradley, Susan Derwin, Connie Sullivan, Stephanie Bain, Amara, Caroline Frank, Leafy Café,

Deena Ensworth, Jennifer Simmons, Katie Vagnino, Jackie Natale, Christi Razzi, Hilary Yeager, Katie Auyer, Janine M., Petra B. Wynbrandt, Steph, Lisa Jacobson, Nicole, Amy Harris, Tanya Solomon, Lexie Creager, Brenda Pfahni, Chris, Carmel, Hallie Andrew, Hisham K., Melanie Anderson, Gail Rush, Michelle Carr, William Broome, Jen Meister, Jayme Catalano, Lauren Barlow, Jonathan Auyer, Gretchen Manzer, Gladys Hills, Scott B., Jay Astafa, Renee Bessette, Naomi, Chris Moffa, Dayle Roberts, and Deeya Pavelle.

Sincerest blessings to those who treated me to meals and provided shelter, showers, and great company throughout the journey: Jim, Ami, Deeya, Dayle, Dave L. Jan L., Karen S., Mark S., Pam M., Dan F., Dan M., Stage, Johana, Janine M., Bryan M., Sarah C., Damien, Ed, Dan H., Alex G., Daniela N., Elisa D., Jon T., Corey G., Liz J., Sarah S., Steve S., Ryan D., Michele R., The Cohen Family, Anna F., The McCullough Family, Adam M., Alec D., Adam L., Nick P., Zoë E., Chris M., Vance, Issa O., Laeticia B., Compassion Over Killing, Uncle Chip, Aunt Nancy, Chris Z., Christina, Rudy, Eric M., Jessica G., Morgan, Clark D., Ryan H., Jennifer F., Thomas S., Kate S., Andrew J., Chris, Michelle, Karen M., Brody, Cindy F., Chevy, Penny, Laney, Vanessa A., Kolene A., Jon D., Nicole G., Chris T., Melanie P., Kim A., Steven A., Kevin S., Katie O., Eric M., Chris S., Christina K., Al K., Sarah, Craig W., The Wilkins Family, Rusty B., Mike R., Todd, Jamey S., Mario C., Tanner O., Megan, Michael, Marisa, James, the staff at Tree of Life in AZ, Paul G., Christina, Nick, Mike S., Jack, Meghan, JJ, Kristan R., Ilsa H., Kayle M., Mandi H., Dave H., Connie S., Joe R., Jose A., *The Vegan Zombie* crew, HappyCow.net, and Miguel D.

Finally, thank you to all of my social media friends and supporters, to all of you who I've only ever "met" through the interwebs, and to YOU for picking up a copy of this book and following along on a journey that quite literally changed my life. I appreciate you.

Contact

KEEP UP WITH KRISTIN

WillTravelForVeganFood.com

KristinLajeunesse.com

Facebook.com/wtfveganfood

YouTube.com/wtfveganfood

Instagram & Twitter: @wtfveganfood

Kristin@wtfveganfood.com

For a complete list of every restaurant Kristin visited, including reviews about each, visit wtfveganfood.com/where-ive-been.

View thousands of photos that chronicle Kristin's journey on Instagram at @wtfveganfood and on Facebook at Facebook.com/wtfveganfood.

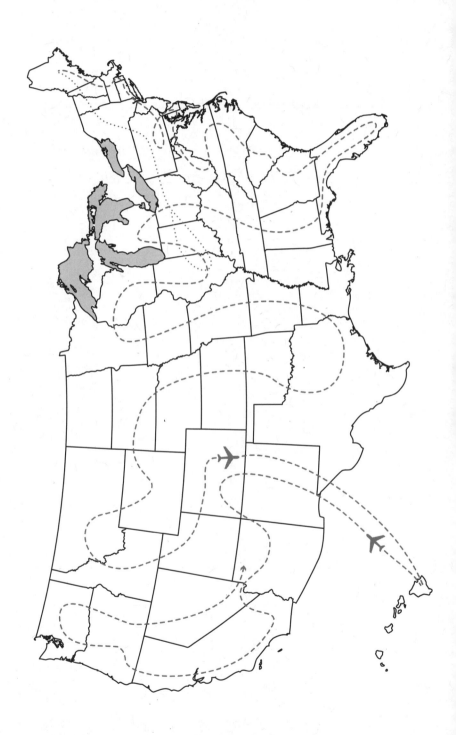